Cinema After Deleuze

D1610001

Deleuze Encounters

Series Editor: Ian Buchanan, Professor of Critical and Cultural Theory, Cardiff University, UK.

The *Deleuze Encounters* series provides students in philosophy and related subjects with concise and accessible introductions to the application of Deleuze's work in key areas of study. Each book demonstrates how Deleuze's ideas and concepts can enhance present work in a particular field.

Series titles include:

Philosophy After Deleuze
Joe Hughes

Political Theory After Deleuze
Nathan Widder

Theology After Deleuze
Kristien Justaert

Cinema After Deleuze

RICHARD RUSHTON

Deleuze Encounters

continuum

Continuum International Publishing Group

The Tower Building	80 Maiden Lane
11 York Road	Suite 704
London	New York
SE1 7NX	NY 10038

www.continuumbooks.com

British Library Cataloguing-in-Publication Data
A catalogue record for this book is available from the British Library.

ISBN: HB: 978-1-4411-6338-7
PB: 978-0-8264-3892-8

Library of Congress Cataloging-in-Publication Data
Rushton, Richard.
Cinema after Deleuze : Deleuze encounters/Richard Rushton.
p. cm.
Includes bibliographical references and index.
ISBN 978-1-4411-6338-7 (hardcover : alk. paper) –
ISBN 978-0-8264-3892-8 (pbk. : alk. paper) –
ISBN 978-1-4411-8288-3 (ebook pdf : alk. paper) –
ISBN 978-1-4411-1199-9 (ebook epub : alk. paper)
1. Motion pictures–Philosophy.
2. Deleuze, Gilles, 1925–1995–Criticism and interpretation. I. Title.
PN1995.R865 2012
791.4301–dc23
2011031698

Typeset by Deanta Global Publishing Services, Chennai, India
Printed and bound in India

Contents

Acknowledgements

Many thanks to Gary Bettinson, Jonathan Munby and Lucy Bolton for giving me access to hard-to-find DVD and VHS copies of films I discuss in the book. Generous thanks to my colleague Nick Gebhardt for his fruitful discussions. Thanks to my Deleuzian friends: Felicity Colman, Barbara Kennedy, Michael Goddard, Patricia Pisters, David Martin-Jones, Bill Marshall, Anna Powell and Will Brown.

1

What Questions does Deleuze's Philosophy of Cinema Answer?

What are the Questions?

What Can Cinema Do?

In his two books on cinema Gilles Deleuze does not seek the essence of cinema (Deleuze, 1986, 1989). As a result, the question he asks of cinema is not the classic one of *what is cinema*? Rather, Deleuze offers many instances and descriptions of what cinema has done, none of which is reducible to a definitive statement of what cinema *is*, nor of what it ought to be. At all times his endeavour is guided by other questions: What has cinema done? What can cinema do? What might cinema become?

In trying to answer such questions Deleuze stays true to the kind of methodology he practices in his other philosophical writings. There, as in the *Cinema* books, he is guided by the process of examining things – whether such things are philosophical propositions, social formations, works of art or literature, models of consciousness and so on – in order to discover ways of answering the question, *how does it work?* In the case of cinema, how it works is only secondarily a question of technology in as much as, for Deleuze, explaining the mechanics of strips of celluloid, of lenses and projectors is not of great significance. Instead, the question of 'how it works' is a question of what kinds of things cinema is able to do, what kinds of meanings and sensations and feelings and effects it can give rise to. In this way, Deleuze's *Cinema* books provide a system of classifications of cinema – what he calls a taxonomy or geology – a series of divisions and types by means of which various films and filmmakers can be characterized and understood.

Why might a philosopher undertake such a project? Is Deleuze offering a *philosophy* of cinema? While offering a complex classification of cinematic signs, Deleuze's *Cinema* books are also works of philosophy. Most significant in this respect are his commentaries on and extensive utilization of concepts adapted from the French philosopher, Henri Bergson (1859–1941). These are books that are of great interest to philosophers and I would contend that three of the major commentaries in English devoted to Deleuze's *Cinema* books have tended to emphasize their philosophical stakes – I refer to Rodowick's *Gilles Deleuze's Time Machine*, Ronald Bogue's *Deleuze on Cinema*, and Paola Marrati's *Gilles Deleuze: Cinema and Philosophy* (Rodowick, 1997; Bogue, 2003; Marrati, 2008). The book you are now reading adopts a somewhat different line of enquiry. Here, my aim is to focus as closely as possible on what Deleuze writes about specific films and filmmakers for, against myriad efforts to define what Deleuze's philosophy of cinema might be, I am concentrating on a more 'nuts and bolts' approach to films and filmmakers.

Does this mean that the present book is unphilosophical or even anti-philosophical? Certainly not. As will become clear in the pages that follow, the best way to come to terms with the philosophical stakes of the *Cinema* books is to *examine the films themselves.* These films will not be understood by way of masterly philosophical explanations that account for those films – or worse, the films will not prove the validity of a Deleuzian philosophical system. Rather, the films themselves provide their own philosophies; the films are in themselves philosophical. This, I believe, is one of the primary aims of Deleuze's *Cinema* books and certainly a chief aim of this book. Therefore, let's get things straight: Deleuze does not invent a philosophy with which to account for cinema. Rather, cinema provides its own philosophies for which Deleuze himself tries to account in the *Cinema* books.

All the same, there are important philosophical underpinnings in the *Cinema* books. These underpinnings can be reduced to four key terms: image, movement, time and history.

What is an Image?

Deleuze discovers an understanding of the word 'image' which he inventively imports from Bergson and which is at odds with what we would normally understand as being an image. For Deleuze, an image is not a representation or secondary copy of something – there is no sense of image as *imitation* or *mimesis* in the *Cinema* books. Instead, to call something an image is to refer to our ways of perceiving and apprehending things. The image of a chair is the chair we see, sit on and understand to be a chair. Thus, there is nothing *behind* the image: there is no 'real' or 'true' chair behind the chair image, no essence of chair for which the chair we see and apprehend would be an image. Rather, the chair image is the only true or real chair we can know.

This understanding of the image has profound consequences for cinema. Deleuze approaches his analyses of films in terms of the images such films have created (for this is what cinema does: it creates images) rather than in terms of the kinds of things such images may represent. Such image types are the ones that this book will trace: the perception-image, action-image, relation-image, crystal-image and much more besides. For the time being, however, it is most important to focus on the major distinction between images drawn by Deleuze, that which thematically divides the two *Cinema* volumes: the *movement-image* and the *time-image*.

For Deleuze, films of the movement-image present an *indirect image of time*, while those of the time-image present a *direct image of time*, or 'a little time in the pure state' (Deleuze 1989, p. 169). These might certainly seem like concise definitions, but they do not go very far towards clarifying what the terms themselves mean. For the movement-image, as might be expected, movement is central to the image. But this centrality should not be misunderstood: the movement-image does not present a series or sequence of images that move. Rather, movement is itself integral to the image. In other words, the movement-image is not composed of images that move, but rather is, as Deleuze will try to call it with some precision, a *movement-image*. In the case of cinema's developments up until World War II, the movement-image, as the dominant mode of the cinematic presentation, assumed the role of charting the world as seen through the eyes of the cinema camera. That is, cinema worked out the ways to tell its stories by means of the camera eye, an eye dissociated from, though also intimately connected with, the human eye. Cinema's great achievement in its first fifty years was to discover an image of the world that was not human. Rather, cinema's perceptions were freed from their ties with human modes of perceiving and apprehending. Hence, Deleuze charts the modes of perception-image, action-image and affection-image, which form the three pillars of the movement-image: perceptions, actions and affections, which become perceptions, actions and images *in themselves*, rather than being the perceptions, actions and affections of human subjects.

And yet, for all its innovations and inventions, the movement-image ultimately came to be defined by one overarching circuit: action and reaction, and it is this circuit which makes the movement-image an *indirect image of time*. Films of the movement-image are typically defined by a problem or set of problems for which a solution must be found. In other words, they are defined by the prospect of the world being 'out of joint' so that ways of putting the world back in its proper shape can be found. Plots are therefore characterized by reactions to a problem and the actions performed deliver a solution to the problem. Characters, plots and films are defined by the actions they perform, that is, by their specific reactions to the problems that confront them.

Why is this an indirect image of time? It is indirect because its form presupposes that the world can, if certain specific actions are performed, be brought to a right, proper and stable order. If that stable order is produced, films of the movement-image imply, then the world might discover its true image and any sense of future change would be annulled. That is why the movement-image presents an indirect image of time *because it implies that change need not happen.*

Time, for Deleuze as much as for Bergson, is *change* or it is nothing at all (for some discussion of this point see Rodowick 1997, pp. 20–3). Therefore, if the movement-image is defined in terms of actions and reactions, which aim to solve problems, films of the time-image find themselves in the position of being unable to find such solutions. In a sense, what we discover in the time-image is a certain inability to work out what the right and proper reposes to a problem are. For most films of the time-image, just working out what the problems might be is more than enough to be confronted with – and as for working out solutions to those problems, this is something that is often beyond the capacities of characters in time-image films. If we are speaking of solutions, then it is not going too far to make some rather brash statements about the movement-image. It might be possible to conceive of the movement-image in terms of what became known under the conditions of National Socialism in Germany during the 1930s and into World War II as the 'final solution'. Deleuze even claims that cinema 'degenerated' into 'a kind of fascism which brought together Hitler and Hollywood' (Deleuze, 1989, p. 164). That is to say, the logic of the movement-image and its determined trajectory is one of trying to discover, in filmic terms, ultimate solutions to the problems facing humanity. Of course, these solutions need not be Nazi ones – the many varieties of the movement-image aspire to myriad solutions, whether these be in the context of Soviet Bolshevism (in the films of Sergei Eisenstein, for example), the American dream (in Elia Kazan, for example) and so on.

Films of the time-image – so presciently figured in auteurs such as Jean Renoir, Orson Welles, Yasujiro Ozu and the Italian Neorealists before and during World War II – simply cannot discover solutions, or actions and reactions, in the ways movement-image films do. Here, there are no final solutions. But they achieve other ends: they dazzle us with their senses of investigating how the world works, of what there is in the world and how the world possesses an irreplaceable beauty and mystery. But why call it a *time*-image? What does Deleuze mean by a 'direct-image of time' or 'a little time in the pure state'? The presentations of the time-image are direct-images of time because they are open to change. The solutions to the problems established by time-image films are not solved in determinate ways – rather, their solutions are left open. This openness has profound consequences for an understanding of time, for it means that, at a first level, the future remains open to change. That is to say, what has happened in the past need not determine ways of conceiving of the future. Furthermore, nor should our ways of conceiving of the present – our ways of coming up with solutions to the problems of our present – hold back the possibilities of the future. In short, a direct image of time is not just one in which the future is left open, but is one in which the past, the present and the future are all open to change. Indeed, as we will discover throughout this book, this might be the major innovation Deleuze adapts from Bergson: a direct image of time, a little time in the pure state, is one in which the past itself will be malleable, not fixed and set for all time. In so far as the past is open to change, then so too are the present and the future.

What is (Film) History?

How do we usually tell ourselves what history is? Perhaps most of us conceive of history in terms of *this* happened, then *this* happened and so on. To put it another way, we say that x happened, and then y happened, and if we understand what history is, then there will be a definite relationship of some sort between x and y. For example, one day, some workers in a factory might be sacked – call this x – while the next day the rest of the workers decide to go on strike – call this y. The relationship between x and y is therefore one of cause and effect: the strike (y) has been caused by, and is thus the effect of, the previous day's sacking of workers (x). For many, I imagine, this is indeed what history is: the joining together of events so as to order and arrange those events – the apocryphal example to which I have alluded here arranges events in terms of cause and effect. This is done in order to discern why certain events have occurred. If we ask 'why did the workers go on strike?' then our answer will be 'because some workers had been sacked to day before'. History, from this perspective, is working out why certain events have followed others.

We might find similar arguments for film history. For example, what are the reasons behind the group of young filmmakers of the late 1950s and 1960s in France who collectively gave rise to what became known as the French 'new wave' (*nouvelle vague*)? There are (so the film history books tell us) any number of reasons: the initiation of the *prime de la qualité* ('subsidy for quality') and the system of *avance sur recettes* ('the advance on receipts') established in France in the late 1950s, or the development of new, lightweight film cameras, which allowed filmmaking to be more portable and easier to set up; or perhaps it all came about because of the inspiration provided by Henri Langlois's *Cinémathèque*; or maybe it was a conscious, filmmaking rebellion against the 'cinema of quality' as fuelled by articles published in *Cahiers du Cinéma*. Perhaps it was all these things (and more). What is certain is that *this* way of understanding history and doing film history is one which looks for the reasons or causes *behind things*. In other words, *y* happened because of *x*.

Do Deleuze's *Cinema* volumes fit into this kind of history? Well, first of all, we might consider that the division between the movement-image and the time-image is a historical one. However, what Deleuze understands by 'history' is not entirely straightforward – it is certainly not a matter of finding relations between cause and effect or of discovering historical 'reasons'. For Deleuze, history can be divided into periods, but there is not necessarily a 'cause' and 'effect' relationship between such periods. What this means for film history is that films can express certain things during certain historical periods that they cannot during other historical periods. For cinema, these historical periods are not technologically determined, for we know that innovations like synchronous sound and the introduction of colour film stock or widescreen formats made available modes of expression that had not been previously possible, but this is not the kind of division Deleuze wants to make. Rather, Deleuze is referring to the capacity for human societies to imagine certain things at certain points in history that they cannot imagine during other historical periods. In this way, Deleuze's historical divisions are indebted to the work of the philosopher, Michel Foucault, especially to his book, *Discipline and Punish*, in which Foucault identifies a transition in the forms of legal punishment at the end of the eighteenth century (Foucault, 1977). Formerly, the punishment of heinous crimes had been carried out directly on the bodies of perpetrators: execution, torture and the like. At the turn of the nineteenth century, however, Foucault identified a significant change: execution and torture began to be replaced by forms of imprisonment and the 'disciplining' of bodies. For Foucault, this meant that societies had begun to imagine discipline and punishment in a different way – it no longer seemed correct or right to torture and execute people, for it was now felt that the proper way to treat criminals was by way of imprisonment. To put it simply, this signalled a change in the ways in which people understood the functioning of criminal punishment, and this, for Foucault, constituted a major historical break, a significant division between historical periods.

It is this kind of historical break which guides Deleuze's understanding of the division between the movement-image and the time-image. The movement-image refers to a specific way in which cinema functioned at a certain point in history, whereas the time-image indicates another way of understanding how cinema functions. The turning point for Deleuze is World War II: films made before World War II are films of the movement-image and those made after the war are those of the time-image. But this is not a hard and fast historical division, for one can easily claim that, if we think of Foucault's *Discipline and Punish*, modes of torture and execution continue to be used today, just as forms of imprisonment were common before the nineteenth century. So too with Deleuze: films of the movement-image did not suddenly end at World War II – indeed, forms of the movement-image continue to be common today – and nor did the time-image simply begin at that point. Rather, what Deleuze tries to emphasize is that the movement-image and the time-image constitute *different modes of filmic expression*, and that the time-image constitutes a different way of conceiving cinema that had not been dominant or typical before World War II. In short, therefore, Deleuze's distinction between the movement-image and the time-image is a historical one, but in making that distinction he is pointing to a very specific kind of 'history'.

How exactly, therefore, are we to read what happens in the *Cinema* books? Is the time-image an 'improvement' of the movement-image? This is a very tricky question to answer – along with it we might ask whether imprisonment offers a better form of punishment than execution and torture. My answer is this: the time-image is *different from* the movement-image, but the time-image is not necessarily better than or an improvement of the movement-image. To put it another way, there might be another kind of image, one that will come to us in the future (or which might even be with us today) and offer another significantly different mode of cinematic expression. Is it important to know whether such a form of expression will be better or worse than the time-image (or better or worse than the movement-image, for that matter)? I think we should try to approach the *Cinema* volumes in terms of classification: Deleuze tries to classify an enormous variety of films and trying to characterize what is particular and significant about specific films and filmmakers is the task he pursues. The task of trying to discern which types of filmmaking are better than others is precisely *not* what the *Cinema* volumes are about. Instead, as Deleuze claims at one point, 'The cinema is always as perfect as it can be' (1986, p. x).

What are Spiritual Automata?

At first sight, for those who are at least a little familiar with Deleuze's *Cinema* books, this question – what are *spiritual automata*? – might seem like one that is only distantly important. Yet, quite to the contrary, I would claim that the stakes of spiritual automata are absolutely crucial for an understanding of Deleuze's approach to cinema. It is worth spending a little time establishing just what this notion is.

First of all, a 'spiritual automaton' is just that: a machine or mechanical device that is endowed with spirit; a thing that thinks (an 'automated spirit'). And this might be about as close as Deleuze gets to defining what cinema is: for cinema is itself a 'spiritual automaton', a machine endowed with a spiritual life, a machine that thinks. And yet, cinema should not be seen as unique in this respect for Deleuze believes that the notion of a spiritual automaton ought to be regarded as a model for thought as such. In other words, thinking should not be conceived as something undertaken by humans or only by humans – or to put it another way, humans should not believe it is they who are the origin of thought. Or, again to rephrase this notion, humans need not believe that thoughts are 'theirs', that they in some way 'own' their thoughts or that thoughts only occur because they 'have' them. Rather, thoughts exist independently of the human beings who have them. It is this independence of thoughts – that thoughts are 'out there' – that Deleuze emphasizes with the notion of the spiritual automaton.

Deleuze borrows the notion of a spiritual automaton from one of his other great philosophical influences: Benedict De Spinoza (1632–77). Deleuze claims that Spinoza's concern in generating these arguments for a spiritual automaton were in the hope that such a notion would differentiate itself from Descartes' famous *Cogito* – 'I think, therefore, I am' – which placed the thoughts of human beings not just at the origin of thought but also at the origin of the knowable universe (see Bogue, 2003, p. 166). For Descartes, therefore, that is what thinking is: thoughts are the products of the human mind. As a result, thoughts or ideas can be discerned by their clarity and distinctness, which is to say that ideas or thoughts can be discerned by how clearly they appear before or 'in' the human mind. Spinoza wanted to challenge such conceptions. His argument runs something like this: thoughts cannot be discerned by how clearly they appear before the mind. Rather, ideas or concepts can only be understood by virtue of how they are *in themselves*. That is to say, thoughts can be discerned by virtue of how well they express themselves – such, at any rate, is Deleuze's argument on this point (see Deleuze, 1992, pp. 151–4). Ideas are quite capable of expressing themselves, as it were, and they do not need to appear before the mind of human beings so as to be interpreted or decoded to be considered ideas. Rather, ideas or thoughts can express themselves *autonomously* – thoughts quite simply are, in themselves, spiritual automata: autonomous expressions of spirit.

The second point to take from Deleuze's Spinozist interpretation is this: the only thoughts we have *come from the outside*. Ideas or thoughts, so this argument goes, do not come from 'within' us. Rather, they are the result of the effect of other bodies on our own (see Deleuze, 1988, pp. 73–76). The influence on Deleuze of the Scottish philosopher, David Hume, is also evident in this respect, for the mind or the 'subject' is here regarded as a product of the *impressions* made by objects and events upon the mind and which, as a product of those sensations and its attendant associations, come to form the mind as such (see Olkowski, 1999, pp. 106–108). In other words, the thoughts we have do not originate 'in' us or in our minds. Rather, they are the product of the sensations, objects and events with which we come into contact.

Now, as far as cinema goes, we must consider that films offer precisely the kinds of sensations and events that can give rise to thought. In fact, cinema might just offer something akin to a perfect example of the way this Deleuzian process functions: while at the cinema, when watching a film, we can drop all preconceptions, forget about the world 'outside', forget our pasts or troubles and 'clear our minds'. Then, as the film unfolds in front of us, we can fill our minds with the most fantastical impressions and sensations. When writing on cinema, Georges Duhamel once famously exclaimed 'I can no longer think what I want to think. My thoughts have been replaced by moving images' (see Deleuze, 1989, p. 166). Duhamel meant this as a criticism, but Deleuze (following Walter Benjamin in this respect) takes it as a claim of highest praise. What he argues is that what is most valuable about cinema is precisely that it *turns me away from the thoughts I own*. Instead, it introduces thoughts that are not mine; it makes me experience the act of thinking as something which comes from the outside, external to me.

Ultimately, this insight might even be Deleuze's most valuable one concerning cinema. If we consider that, when adapting Bergson's concept of the 'image', Deleuze argues that there are no images *of* things, but rather that images *are* things, then this means we are not the origin of images. In other words, *we* do not have images of things, but instead, what we can call images occur as the combination of things and our apprehension of those things. And much the same goes for thinking: thoughts are not things we have, which means we are not at the origin of thought. Rather, thoughts occur when they come into contact with us. What happens at the cinema, therefore, can be considered a product of what comes into contact with us in any given film. And this is central to Deleuze's consideration of cinema (and to his philosophy as a whole). What is most crucial is that, while we are watching a film, we are traversed by sensations, affects and perceptions *that are not ours*. Because of this, while watching a film, we are able to encounter things we have never encountered before. In other words, while at the cinema, we are able to encounter that which is genuinely *new*. To be able to encounter the genuinely new is what is most valuable for Deleuze's view of cinema.

2

The Movement-Image (I): Griffith, Eisenstein, Gance, Lang

The Movement-Image

Deleuze begins *Cinema 1: The Movement-Image* with a veritable avalanche of terms and philosophical arguments, especially those relating to what he considers Bergson's three theses on movement. To call the opening pages of the book 'daunting' is something of an understatement. I would therefore encourage readers of this book to look elsewhere to unpick those opening pages – or better still, to go slowly and carefully through those pages themselves (see Bogue, 2003, pp. 11–39; Marrati, 2008, pp. 6–43; Rushton, 2011a, pp. 126–147) for, as I stated in Chapter 1, I am determined to go to the films and filmmakers themselves.

First of all, however, Deleuze gives us three terms to initially work with, and these are terms that are familiar in film studies: frame, shot and montage.

(a) *Frame*. Deleuze uses the notion of the frame in much the same way as any film scholar might. The frame, to start with, refers to those individual 'frames' of the cinematic image that are registered on a celluloid strip and projected at 24 frames per second. But the frame also refers to the 'framing' a cinema camera selects: the camera 'cuts out' a certain part of the world, that part of the world bounded by the four sides of the rectangle which will then be projected onto a screen during the screening of a film. In other words, the cinema camera 'frames' what it sees and captures and such framing is a basic aspect of cinema for Deleuze. (For a more extensive discussion of Deleuze's elucidation of the 'frame', see Bogue, 2003, pp. 42–4.)

(b) *Shot*. A shot is the combination of frames that make up what in English is called a 'take'. There is no equivalent for 'take' in French; rather, *plan* means both 'shot' and 'take'. *Un plan* is therefore both spatial and durational: a shot can convey depth, as in the distinction between a close-up, a medium shot or a long shot; while a shot also unfolds in time; i.e., shots can be extremely short or long. (Typically in English the latter is referred to as a 'take'.) These abilities of the shot lead Deleuze to claim that 'The shot is the movement-image' (Deleuze, 1986, p. 22), for it is only when the cinema develops a conception of the shot, and especially of the relations between shots (see Bonitzer, 1982), that cinema as movement-image is born. It is the shot that gives movement to cinema and by virtue of which the movement-image is born.

(c) *Montage*. Montage, as is well known, is the division of shots, the cutting between shots, but even more importantly, the *linking* between shots. If we consider editing as the cutting from one shot to another, then montage is a matter of putting shots together into some kind of form or structure. It is montage that allows Deleuze to bring together the three basic components of the cinematic image:

● The frame is the determination of a closed system (or 'set' as Deleuze calls them) – that is, a part of the world that is framed, cut out and cut off from the rest of the world.

● The shot then links these separate parts and puts them together so as to endow them with movement. If we think of the frame in terms of the strip of celluloid, then we can think of the shot as that act of movement that brings together and synthesizes those frames such that they move.

- Montage is the capacity for uniting these elements so as to constitute a whole. It is by way of montage that a sense of unity or wholeness is given to the movement-image.

D. W. Griffith

It is in this way that Deleuze builds up to the first major filmmaker of the movement-image: D. W. Griffith. It is Griffith who first conceived of a way of building up the separate components of the cinema – its frames and shots – to develop a unique vision of the whole by way of montage. Deleuze writes:

> Griffith conceived of the composition of movement-images as an organization, an organism, a great organic unity. This was his discovery. The organism is, first of all, unity in diversity, that is, a set of differentiated parts; there are men and women, town and country, rich and poor, North and South, interiors and exteriors, etc. These parts are taken in binary relationships which constitute a *parallel alternate montage*, the image of one part succeeding another according to a rhythm (Deleuze, 1986, p. 30).

Very few today doubt the significance of Griffith's innovations, for it was he who laid the foundations of cinematic form in ways that are still dominant today. Deleuze is no exception here, for he acknowledges Griffith's role in giving films a sense of the whole.

This sense of the whole – of the organization, an organic unity – emerges forcefully in Griffith's early masterpiece *A Corner in Wheat* (1909). Here, as Tom Gunning has deftly explained, Griffith's use of parallel editing brings together, by way of association and contrast, three narrative strands. The first involves a generic farmer who toils, it is implied, for long hours sowing and harvesting his wheat crops. The second involves a rich speculator, the 'Wheat King', who thrives on grain speculation, and who during the film corners the wheat market. The third narrative strand involves the consumers who, in the wake of the Wheat King's speculation, are now forced to pay double the price for a loaf of bread. The result of this, of course, is that many can no longer afford their daily bread. As Gunning claims, 'Parallel editing becomes in this film a form of economic analysis' (Gunning, 1991, p. 244): the speculator grows enormously wealthy, while the farmer and the consumers are left in dire poverty. Even as the Wheat King dramatically meets his end when he falls into one of his own grain elevators, thus courting the possibility of a happy ending, Griffith instead, at the film's end, cuts back to the poor farmer, still struggling, sowing his grain, but now even poorer, for he can no longer afford the horses that assisted him at the film's opening.

Griffith thus brilliantly demonstrates the divisions between rich and poor and masterfully portrays the relations between them, that is, of how the actions of one can have dire consequences for the other. As Gunning writes, 'we see a series of disparate scenes of American life, brought together only by their economic relation': producer, consumer and speculator (Gunning, 1991, p. 244). It is in this way that the series of frames and shots – the individual sets which portray the producer, consumer and speculator – are brought together into a meaningful whole by way of montage. As Deleuze claims, this is Griffith's great discovery: to have formulated an organic whole out of the organization of individual sets.

It is the relation between the parallel lines of narrative action that are crucial for understanding Griffith's innovations. And, as Deleuze uncontroversially claims, these can remain separated (as they do in A Corner in Wheat, or most famously in segments of Intolerance [1916] as well as in Broken Blossoms [1919]) or they can converge, as they more often do; that is, the conclusion of the film will entail the coming together of the separate lines of action: the chase in Birth of a Nation [1915], the modern narrative of Intolerance, and the rescue in Way Down East [1920]).

Griffith's other great innovation was the invention of the close-up, of which Deleuze is well aware: 'the close-up', for Griffith, 'endows the objective set with a subjectivity which equals or even surpasses it' (Deleuze, 1986, p. 30). What does Deleuze mean by this? First of all, the close-up endows whatever we have seen with a sense of subjectivity – that is, it endows the situation with the feelings or thoughts of a character. But in doing this, the close-up has the possibility of surpassing what the objective set presents. What Deleuze is trying to say is the objective views of events we can have from a distance (whether a medium shot or long shot) can allow us to comprehend the meaning of the set in an objective way – it can, for example, allow us to clearly discern the distinctions between rich and poor, black and white and so on. But in Griffith's work the close-up, Deleuze claims, can deepen these distinctions by endowing them with a subjective psychology. By way of images such as these we can sense a character's range of affect – indeed, what Deleuze calls the 'affection-image' will become a central tenet of the movement-image (as we shall see in the next chapter).

The famous scenes of Lucy's (Lillian Gish) 'smile' in *Broken Blossoms* are central here. We can all too plainly see her brutal father, 'Battling Burrows', enveloped as he is in a pitiful situation of poverty, as a mean-spirited man who vents his anger on his defenceless daughter. But we can be moved to tears as Gish desperately tries to smile beneath that barrage of abuse: she slowly and carefully places her fingers at the edge of her mouth in an attempt to turn up its ends in a painful imitation of a smile. On the one hand, we see the objective portrayal of poverty and abuse, while with the close-up we obtain a fully realized subjective sense of the feeling of that poverty. Griffith fully exploited the psychological, subjective possibilities of the close-up.

Griffith himself was certain that the close-up was linked with psychological states or imaginings. For example, it was felt that by cutting – alternating – from a man engaged in thought, to a close-up image of his sweetheart, and then cutting back again, the inserted image of his sweetheart would invariably be an image of 'what he was thinking' (on these points see the descriptions in Bordwell, 1982, p. 129). Griffith uses this kind of intercutting extensively in *Birth of a Nation*, so that when Elsie (Lillian Gish) feels she has fallen in love with Cameron, she is portrayed in close-up as 'thinking about him' while parallel images show Cameron returning home. Later in the film (while his sister prepares his 'Ku Klux Klan' robes, no less), Cameron brings Elsie 'into his mind', while intercut images portray Elsie (in close-up once again). The close-up, in conjunction with parallel editing, thus develops the power to display the subjective dimensions of feeling and thinking, powers which the cinema will find irresistible throughout its history.

Eisenstein and Soviet Montage

Sergei Eisenstein takes up the challenge that (for him) Griffith failed to complete: what happens if the relations between the parallel segments of a narrative might result in transformation or change? Beyond Griffith's parallel or convergent montage, Eisenstein puts in place a dialectical form of montage. Again, Deleuze does nothing that might be contrary to accepted versions of film history: Griffith is the master of parallel montage as much as Eisenstein masters what he himself refers to as dialectical montage. If Griffith's convergent montages seem accidental or 'unguided' – that is, if they just happen to happen – then Eisenstein's, on the contrary, are guided by dialectical logic. Deleuze seems to imply that Eisenstein is guided by logical or even spiritual laws of nature or organic formation, and Eisenstein's professed adherence to the law of the 'golden section' (at least so far as *The Battleship Potemkin* [1925] goes; see Eisenstein, 1970) would indicate that Deleuze is most likely correct in this regard.

Deleuze argues that Eisenstein makes dialectics dynamic by transforming opposites. Eisenstein's montages are animated by clashes to the point that, in the wake of Eisenstein's distinction between 'organic unity' and 'pathos', Deleuze claims that the *organic* carves out a great spiral, while the *pathetic* intersects that spiral in order to spark events into action. If the organic points to the laws of growth or progress, then the pathetic indicates those moments or events that spur growth and further progress. For example, the moment at which the progression of events is sparked forwards occurs when the sailors aboard the Potemkin see their meat crawling with maggots: the sailors are forced to stand up to their superiors and instigate a clash with them by virtue of which change will be invoked. It is in this way that the transformation into opposites is brought about; that is, via the dynamics of the clash which we find again and again in Eisenstein's films. To call such clashes 'pathetic' is central to Eisenstein's processes (and of which Deleuze is fully aware), for we, as viewers of the film, are inspired to feel pity for the plight of the characters – for the sailors in *The Battleship Potemkin*, the workers in *Strike* (1924), the revolutionaries in *October* (1928), Martha and the cooperative members in *The General Line* (1929). The moments of pathos are therefore the ones in which we are pushed to imagine what transforming the world would be like. By contrast, with Griffith, we can feel sorrow and pity for a character, but that does not drive us to change the world. For Eisenstein the opposite is the case; if we feel pity for a character, the only way to overcome that pity is to change the world.

In *The Battleship Potemkin* the organic spiral grows and grows, and it is intersected by various moments of pathos – by the death of Vakulinchuck, the climax of pathos on the Odessa Steps and the eventual resolution via the confrontation with another battleship – and we find similar patterns in Eisenstein's other silent films, which are designed to engineer a transformational leap. Much of the emphasis of the transformational leap is occupied by the other great technique Eisenstein modifies from Griffith: the close-up. If the close-up in Griffith's work introduces a subjective dimension to the image, then this is only partly the case for Eisenstein. Far more important is the sense that the close-up in Eisenstein introduces *an absolute change*. 'If it includes a subjectivity', writes Deleuze, 'it is in the sense that consciousness is also a passage into a new dimension' (Deleuze, 1986, p. 35).

How precisely does Eisenstein achieve this passage into a new dimension? 'If the pathetic is development', writes Deleuze, 'it is because it is the development of consciousness itself: it is the leap of the organic which produces an external consciousness of society and its history' (Deleuze, 1986, p. 36). Eisenstein's processes are definitive: where Griffith's montages and close-ups are psychological, Eisenstein's are social, and their aim is to produce revolutionary consciousness. A magnificent display of the way that this process of montage, consciousness and revolution develops occurs in *Strike*. When one of the workers at the factory discovers that a micrometer has gone missing, he decides to go to the factory manager to inform him. When he does so, the manager turns on him and accuses him of having stolen the micrometer. Eisenstein portrays this confrontation with bravura editing patterns in which the manager and the worker confront and provoke each other, to the point where, at times, each of their heads looks as though it will break through the screen. It is this kind of escalation produced by montage which, when combined with the passionate excesses of the close-up, produces precisely the kind of pathos that induces the transformational leap into a social-revolutionary realm. Deleuze's emphasis on the combination of elements – that is, that Eisenstein's use of montage cannot be dissociated from his innovative use of the close-up – places Eisenstein at the forefront of those filmmakers who have explored the relation between film and thought. These issues will be explored in greater detail in Chapter 8.

Abel Gance and French Impressionism

If Griffith sets in motion the movement-image by way of parallel montage, and Eisenstein turns those parallel lines into oppositional or dialectical ones, then it is Gance who explores something akin to the limits of the relation between movement and montage. For Deleuze, Gance's formulations are all explorations of movement, of rhythm and metre. One aim, states Deleuze, is to produce 'a maximum quantity of movement in given space' (Deleuze, 1986, p. 41). Again we should ask: why is this so?

The main reason for the maximizing of movement is to forge a distinction between two types of time. The first, which Deleuze describes as 'the interval as variable present', entails a laying bare of the time of the present, of describing the ways in which time can serve to spatially unite disparate presents. The second type of time explodes this set of presents in order to portray time as an 'open whole', as 'the immensity of future and past'. We should ask other questions here: how does this work and why is it significant?

The first type of time is quite common in Gance's epic films (*La Roue* [1923], *Napoléon* [1927]), where a series of actions or events that occur in spaces far away from each other are united and related; a form of parallel montage, certainly, but with the kinds of strong, poetic overtones that distinguish them from the naturalism of Griffith. For example, there are brilliantly poetic, associational montage sequences in *Napoléon* – when the young Napoleon is escaping from Corsica on a stormy sea on the very same evening that Robespierre has inflamed the Constitutional Assembly by sentencing Danton to the guillotine: the storm at sea is mirrored by the conflagration of the members at the Assembly. Another example will take us up to the second form of time: in *La Roue*, when Norma, trying to escape from her stepfather in order to be secretly married, does not know that it is her stepfather who is driving the train she is using for her escape. Thus, the montage serves to unite these spaces even as they are defined by their separation, and is thus an example of the first type of time (that is, a laying bare of the time of the present). However, Norma's stepfather *does* know she is on the train and, as a result, he tries to sabotage the journey by crashing the train. And so ensues one of Gance's most extreme and most extraordinary montage sequences: here, there is no sense of spaces being brought together in anything like a measured fashion. On the contrary, Gance here unleashes a dimension beyond measure, a mad and furious rushing and intersecting of overlaid, superimposed, dizzying, clashing and dismembering montages as the train speeds towards its doom. This is a time beyond measure – 'the immensity of future and past' – which careers towards death. In this instance, dramatically, the train is spared from crashing by the stepfather's assistant who averts disaster just in time (thus restoring the time of the present).

This example from *La Roue* highlights another aspect of Gance's innovations: the relation between man and machine. For the Russians, the dialectical unity of man and machine was the key to a utopian future (in Vertov, Dovzhenko, as much as Eisenstein, not to mention El Lizzitzky or Tatlin). For the French, however, the conjunction of man and machine would lead to a furious kinetic energy which, if not held in check or mastered, could only lead to death and destruction (the last of the Impressionist films might therefore be Renoir's *La Bête Humaine* [1938]). 'The kinetic union', writes Deleuze, 'between man and machine was to define a new Human Beast' (Deleuze, 1986, p. 43).

And yet, there is a guiding reason behind all this: the mathematical sublime. For Gance, one challenge for man was to contain and understand Nature, but another challenge was to surpass Nature and enter into the incalculable greatness of an uncharted realm. Deleuze argues that, for Gance, inheriting the Romantic legacy of Immanuel Kant's aesthetics, 'thought must attain that which surpasses all imagination, that is, the set of movements as a whole, absolute maximum of movements, absolute movement which is in itself identical to the incommensurable or the measureless, the gigantic, the immense: canopy of the heavens of limitless sea' (Deleuze, 1986, p. 46). For Deleuze, then, this is the goal of Gance's montages: to transfer us from the measured realm of associational montage to the limitless realm of the immeasurable. And it is no doubt true that Gance's most extreme montage formations are beyond the perceptual and conceptual capacities of ordinary human perception so that what he aims for is that which surpasses ordinary human conception, what Deleuze calls 'superimpressions in the soul' (Deleuze, 1986, p. 48). It is in this way that Gance gives to cinema a notion of the sublime.

Fritz Lang and German Expressionism

The silent Germans too have their sublime, but while Gance advocates a mathematical sublime (that of immeasurable number, of infinite movement) for the Germans the sublime is dynamic. It is worth going into some detail on these points, and we must ask ourselves: What constitutes the sublime for Kant and Deleuze? For judgements of the beautiful, argues Kant, the imagination (as a 'faculty' of the mind) finds agreement and harmony with the understanding. To put this another way, if I see – that is, by way of intuition or sensibility – something which I consider beautiful, then the imagination is the faculty that has the power to bring what I have seen (by way of sensibility) into accord with what I can think (by virtue of the understanding). The imagination is thus a link between the senses and the mind, and when the imagination discovers harmony between the senses and the mind, then it has discovered something beautiful. Furthermore, when I see something beautiful, I might say that it feels 'right', it seems as though 'things are meant to be that way' because my faculties are harmoniously conjoined. This feeling is one of pleasure.

The sublime occurs, on the contrary, when the imagination exceeds reason – and for the sublime, it is a matter of the relation between the imagination and reason (rather than understanding). Reason, for Kant, strives for unity, so that when the imagination is confronted with a feeling which goes beyond what can be contained by any conceivable unity, then the imagination is awed and encounters the feeling of the sublime. As a result, the feeling of the sublime is not an invocation of harmony or accord. Rather, the sublime is the product of a *conflict* between the imagination and reason, for the imagination cannot make what it sees (by way of sensibility) 'fit' with the unity to which reason aspires. The feeling engendered by the sublime is one of *pain* rather than pleasure.

We have seen how this painful excess works for Gance: it functions mathematically, by way of number and movement which ends in the overwhelming destruction of death. For the German Expressionists – especially Lang – the dynamic sublime gives rise to feelings of devastating awe. As Deleuze puts it, the sublime of the Expressionists produces an 'intensity which is raised to such a power that it dazzles or annihilates organic being, strikes terror into it' (Deleuze, 1986, p. 53). The dynamic sublime is utterly overwhelming.

Few commentators would disagree with such a diagnosis. Tom Gunning, for example, in his brilliant study of Lang, argues that his films are guided by a 'destiny machine' (the title of Lang's 1921 film, *Der müde Tod*, is typically translated into English as 'Destiny'). From out of this destiny machine, Gunning traces three key themes. The first of these entails *disenchantment with the world*. As Gunning argues, Lang's *Die Nibelungen* (1924) chronicles 'the disenchantment of a magical world and the apocalyptic consequences of that betrayal' (Gunning, 2000, p. 35). Deleuze himself paints these issues in much more dramatic tones, claiming that these films are about a 'dark, swampy life into which everything plunges' (Deleuze, 1986, p. 50). In the first part of *Die Nibelungen* ('Siegfried'), the mythical, magical hero Siegfried is betrayed and killed. The second part of the film ('Kreimhilde's Revenge') charts the painful consequences of this betrayal: the fatal destruction of a way of life and the entrance into a death-world of complete obliteration. Siegfried Kracauer calls it 'an orgy of destruction' (Kracauer, 1947, p. 92). (This is heady stuff indeed, but one should not underestimate the astonishing madness of 'Kreimhilde's Revenge' and its relation to the unhealed German wounds of World War I.)

What can be the point of all this death and destruction (and we find it in various ways in *Der müde Tod*, in the *Mabuse* films [*Dr Mabuse: The Gambler* (1922) and *The Testament of Dr Mabuse* (1933)], as well as *M* [1931])? For Kant, the pain of the sublime is not *mere* pain. Rather, in the end, the sublime produces a pleasure that can be associated with awe – as Kant puts it, the sublime produces 'a feeling of being unbounded' (Kant, 1987, p. 98 [§23]); it is something that 'expands the soul', we might say. Deleuze himself argues that 'the sublime is engendered within us in such a way that it prepares for a higher finality' (Deleuze, 1984, p. 52). Furthermore, by virtue of the sublime 'we discover that which is fundamental to our destiny (ibid.). Ultimately, then, the pain of the sublime prepares us for a greater future – or at least for the conception of a greater future. Again reading with Deleuze, the sublime 'arouses a thinking faculty by which we feel superior to that which annihilates us, to discover in us a supra-organic spirit which dominates the whole organic life of things: then we lose our fear knowing that our spiritual "destination" is truly invincible' (Deleuze, 1984, p. 53). In other words, the Expressionist evocation of the sublime presents us with a world bathed in the fury of destruction only so that we might discover a higher world and a better way of life. The disenchantment of the world thus entails its potential re-enchantment. We can see the operation of this kind of cycle – in which the world is redeemed – in the denouement of *Metropolis* (1927).

The second point that Gunning emphasizes in Lang's German films is the theme of *the dead caught up with the living*: 'one of the master themes of Lang's films throughout his career [. . .] has been the difficulties of the return of the dead to the world of the living' (Gunning, 2000, p. 40). For Deleuze, this is a central aspect of the Expressionist aesthetic, the dead or inanimate forms which are every bit as alive as those beings that possess organic life. If, as we have discovered, Eisenstein worked towards a dialectical unity of man and machine, while in Gance the conjoining of man and machine unleashes kinetic fury, for the Expressionists, man and machine are cut from the same cloth. For Lang, Deleuze argues, there is a 'pre-organic vitality' which is common to machines as well as organisms, to the animate and the inanimate. Hence the line between the world of the living and the world of the dead is blurred or non-existent. The demonically possessed scribblings of Mabuse, the robot Maria (not to mention the workers and the many other machines) in *Metropolis*, even the chalked 'M' of *M* – these have a life of their own. But it is more than anywhere in the mises-en-scenes of these films that the inanimate comes to life: the skyscrapers and the workers' underworld of *Metropolis*, the cragged castles and plains of *Die Nibelungen* and in the streets, buildings, corridors, alley ways, darkened rooms and underground cells of *M*. (Clearly other Expressionist films are central here too for Deleuze, from *The Cabinet of Doctor Caligari* [1920] through Murnau's *Nosferatu* [1922] and *The Last Laugh* [1924].)

Deleuze claims, with reference to Wilhelm Worringer's analyses of Gothic art (Worringer, 1957), that in German Expressionism, 'diagonals and cross-diagonals tend to replace the horizontal and the vertical' (Deleuze, 1986, p. 52) so that all becomes angles, bends, odd shapes and dead ends. Deleuze's point is that this architecture is as much 'alive' as any of the organically animate beings present in these films, while organic life – especially of the human variety – tends to get sucked into, consumed or drowned (almost literally in *Metropolis*) in these monumental structures. What this all amounts to for Deleuze is the presentation in these films of '*the non-organic life of things*' (Deleuze, 1986, p. 50). Curiously, perhaps, this eerie concatenation of the non-organic life of things gives rise to a feeling of the sublime and it is on this final point that Deleuze's analysis will hinge. He writes that the proliferation of non-organic yet living elements (what we might nowadays simply call the 'undead') culminates in:

> a *non-psychological life of the spirit*, which no longer belongs either to Nature or to our organic individuality, which is the divine part in us, the spiritual relationship in which we are alone with God as light. Thus, the soul seems to rise up again towards the light (Deleuze, 1986, p. 54).

The aim therefore of the Expressionists is to give birth to a new spiritual life, and such is the third point Gunning attributes to Lang's films: the march of destiny and the struggle against that seemingly determined fate. The fate-driven elements that wreak havoc and vengeance upon the Earth – Hagen, Mabuse, Rotwang and the robot Maria and Beckert – these are the figures of darkness, driven or determined by fate, whose only destiny is death. If these are the forces of darkness, then they are counteracted by the force of light and the play of light, and it is indeed the play of light and dark that becomes the defining characteristic of German Expressionism.

The most extreme point on the scale of darkness is, of course, that point at which there is no light. If this is the limit of darkness, a zero degree of light, then any emanation of light out of that darkness will be pulsations of intensity, of *a* life, of a potential for redemption, a flicker or glimmer of hope. This harsh relation between dark and light – the chiaroscuro central to Expressionism – is thus figured by Deleuze as a way of opening us onto the infinite divinity of the sublime. Such were the grand dreams of silent cinema: the dream that both humankind and the world itself could be raised to a higher level of being.

3

The Movement-Image (II): Ford and Kazan

Perception, Action, Affection

Central to Deleuze's conception of the movement-image is that all images are subject to 'universal variation'. All is movement and all is image and, as such, no image is ever static, instead the image continually changes and varies. For Deleuze, this continual movement ushers in nothing less than a new way of conceiving the universe and cinema makes this way of apprehending things clear. This way of conceiving, Deleuze argues, is inspired by Bergson's philosophy and, by being Bergsonian, cinema directly brings into question the dominant ways in which the universe has been conceived. What cinema brings into the open is a critique of phenomenology and other subject-centred philosophies.

Most modern philosophies – certainly from Descartes onwards – have conceived of the universe in terms of a static snapshot; that is, they are based on the notion that, if we stop all things from moving, then measure the coordinates and the relationships between these static things, we will have a map of the universe which puts all things in their rightful place. One way to conceive of this might be in terms of the invention of linear perspective in painting: a mapping of the universe from a central point in which all rays of light converge on the singular observing eye of the mathematician-painter, a world mapped out and clearly divided into distinct spatial relationships. Of course, such a way of seeing is also replicated by photography, whereby rays of light are captured and frozen with the observable distances between things fixed and framed accordingly. Deleuze is keen to point out that all of these ways of picturing the world have left out something essential: movement. And it is cinema which gives to us a conception of the universe to which movement has been restored.

Deleuze forcefully argues that cinema can demonstrate the faults of traditional, subject-centred philosophies. Crucially, Deleuze opposes Bergson's philosophy with phenomenological approaches. Phenomenology, a philosophical movement which emerged during the same historical period as Bergson's philosophy, advocates a view of the world that remains static and based on the visions of a non-moving, anchored subject or eye. For Bergson's philosophy, on the contrary, movement is fundamental. Bergson's philosophical breakthrough is encapsulated by his retort to the phenomenological claim that 'consciousness is consciousness of something'. The task for the phenomenologist is to discern the ways in which I become conscious of things; that is, I take my consciousness as the centre of the task at hand and, by enquiring into my consciousness and the somethings which appear to it, I can discern in what ways and under which effects I become conscious of things. In short, I am at the origin of those things which appear to my consciousness. Bergson defuses such claims by declaring that, rather than 'consciousness is consciousness of something' that 'consciousness is something'. This means that my consciousness is no longer at the origin and centre of things, for it instead means that my consciousness is in things, it is produced by the things with which it comes into contact. Exactly what Bergson means here – and precisely what it is that Deleuze takes from him – require a little unpacking, but they are absolutely crucial for an understanding of what cinema is for Deleuze.

Cinema is crucial for this notion of perception in movement, a form of perception and comprehension that is always changing and shifting. If we conceive of photography as putting into play a phenomenological conception of the universe – with the camera eye at the centre of that vision of things – then cinema puts into play a moving image, a moving image in which the centre of the image is also constantly in movement: a camera which moves, editing which constantly shifts the centre of perspective and emphasis of the shot, an emphasis which might at one moment be seen from one character's perspective, at the next moment from another's, then from the perspective of no character at all. What the invention of the three basic techniques of cinema we saw in the last chapter (frame, shot and montage) results in is a conception of the universe as universal movement.

If the world or the universe is in a state of universal variation then how is it that we are able to distinguish or make sense of anything? According to Deleuze's analysis, 'living beings' – including and especially human beings – can capture or absorb perceptions and rays of light in ways that make them 'centres of indetermination'. At this centre is the brain, but the brain is merely a conduit of communication, 'no more than', as Bergson so aptly puts it, 'a kind of central telephonic exchange' (Bergson, 1988, p. 30). As the centre of this exchange, the brain receives the stimuli of perception and responds to those stimuli accordingly. In short, the universe consists of a massive array of things – images – each of which has the capacity to act on everything else, and in which the definitive state of things is one in which everything is acting in relation to everything else. 'Everything', states Deleuze, 'that is to say every image, is indistinguishable from its actions and reactions: this is universal variation' (Deleuze, 1986, p. 58). It is from these founding theses that Deleuze invents the three most important image sub-categories of the movement-image: the *perception-image*, the *action-image* and the *affection-image*.

What, first of all, is a 'perception'? Perception occurs when stimuli intersect a living being – that is, when stimuli cross the path of a 'centre of indetermination'. If the arc traced by a bird as it flies through the sky intersects with my capacity for vision, then I can say that I 'see' this bird, I have *perceived* it. In fact, it might be that very little actually 'intersects' our perceptual faculties. I might 'see' this bird, but myriad other stimuli will go by entirely unnoticed by me: I fail to notice the cloud formation or the sunlight on the hills behind the bird; I fail to notice that gentle westerly breeze and the way it rustles some nearby leaves; but, yes, I do hear that dog barking incessantly! In other words, any 'centre of indetermination' will perceive *some things* – it will be intersected by some things – while a whole host of other things will pass by entirely unnoticed and, thus, will not be perceived. Deleuze describes this in the following way, quoting from Bergson: 'Living beings "allow to pass through them, so to speak, those external influences which are indifferent to them; the others isolated, become 'perceptions' by their very isolation"' (Deleuze, 1986, pp. 61–2). Or as he puts it even more emphatically elsewhere: 'We perceive the thing, minus that which does not interest us as a function of our needs' (ibid., p. 63).

Cinema is again crucial here, for it demonstrates to us this function of perception by way of what Deleuze calls 'perception-images'. As one commentator puts it, '[t]he operation of perception-images is framing' (Marrati, 2008, p. 35), and this is indeed how perception comes to cinema: the camera 'cuts out' a certain part of the world, and that which is framed is what is perceived. The frame cuts out a certain space and duration of perception and thus a 'perception-image' is created. To repeat Deleuze's claim from above: 'Everything, that is to say every image, is indistinguishable from its actions and reactions: this is universal variation' (Deleuze, 1986, p. 58). Its action is, first of all, the perception-image, the action upon the camera screen of that which is framed, the action of the stimuli which intersects the camera eye itself as a 'centre of indetermination'. We might characterize the perception-image as 'what the camera sees'; that is, as the action of light upon the camera and its subsequent projection onto the screen. Allied with this action, however, is the potential for a reaction. It is this capacity for response or reaction that Deleuze calls the *action-image*.

If the perception-image results from cinema's 'cutting out' of a part of the world, then the action-image arises as a response to this cutting out. We can conceive of the perception/action relation in the following way. If someone strikes me with his hand, then I might be inclined to respond to this strike with a strike of my own, or I could exclaim, 'stop that!' or 'why did you do that?' In short, in response to an action performed on me, as something registered by perception,

I can respond in various ways by producing an action of one sort or another. Such is the basis for the relation between a *perception* and an *action* as Deleuze describes them.

What, then, is an action-*image* in so far as such an image pertains to cinema? Deleuze argues that any perception-image will automatically contain possible responses to it, as he claims: every image 'is indistinguishable from its actions and reactions'. Therefore, the action-image is an outcome of the responses to the perception-image. '[P]erceiving things here where they are, I grasp the "virtual action" that they have on me, and simultaneously the "possible action" that I have on them, in order to associate me with them or to avoid them' (Deleuze, 1986, pp. 64–5). A perception-image, therefore, is a form of registering, of receiving stimuli. Built into that reception is also the sense of what to do with what has been received and it is this possibility for action that leads to the action-image. If the perception-image is the reception of stimuli, then the action-image is the response to that reception.

If someone strikes me with his hand, then I might be inclined to respond to this strike with a strike of my own. And yet, perhaps the strike against me will cause me to clutch my shoulder, the place where I was struck, as I feel a sharp pain shuddering through my body. My response will be delayed, which is to say I will not strike back immediately. Indeed, there will always be some sort of gap between a perception and an action, however small. This gap between perception and action is what Bergson and Deleuze call *affection*. In cinema, between the perception-image and the action-image there is the *affection-image*. As Deleuze so evocatively describes it:

> There is an in-between. Affection is what occupies the interval, what occupies it without filling it or filling it up. It surges in the centre of indetermination, that is to say in the subject . . . . It is a coincidence of subject and object, or the way in which the subject feels itself 'from the inside' (Deleuze, 1986, p. 65).

Later in *Cinema 1* (in Chapter 6) Deleuze focuses on the affection-image and its relationship with the face. The face is crucial for the conception of the affection-image in so far as the face is a zone which does not so much respond to stimuli with actions or reactions, but instead is a zone upon which is registered the affect of things. When I am struck on the shoulder, the pain certainly surges in that shoulder, but it will also be registered by the grimace on my face, a scrunching up of the eyes and a slightly agonized opening of my mouth: the affects are registered by my face. The face is a zone of affection and it will come as no surprise that cinema has found such a repository of emotional splendour and magnificence in the close-up of the face.

The face is this organ-carrying plate of nerves that has sacrificed most of its global motility and gathers or expresses in a free way all kinds of tiny local movements, which the rest of the body usually keeps hidden (Deleuze, 1986, pp. 87–8).

These, therefore, are the three main divisions on the movement-image: the *perception-image*, the *action-image* and *the affection-image*.

The Large Form of the Action-Image: John Ford

The most important form of the movement-image – certainly in so far as it has been central to the success of Hollywood cinema – is what Deleuze calls 'the large form of the action-image'. It is in the 'large form' that perception, action and affection enter into relations that best define the operations of the movement-image. And yet, additionally, Deleuze confidently characterizes the 'large form' as a form devoted to *realism*. We should not confuse this kind of realism with that advocated by André Bazin or associated with Italian neorealism, British 'kitchen sink' dramas of the 1960s or myriad other provocative claims for 'realist' approaches to cinema. Rather, what Deleuze means by realism is what is typically referred to as 'classical Hollywood realism', a series of conventions perfected by Hollywood films, which create a very convincing illusion of reality. It is this systematic, conventional approach to realism to which Deleuze refers. From such a perspective Deleuze specifically characterizes the realism of the 'large form':

What constitutes realism is simply this: milieux and modes of behaviour, milieux which actualize and modes of behaviour which embody. The action-image is the relation between the two and all the varieties of this relation. It is this model which produces the universal triumph of the American cinema (Deleuze, 1986, p. 141).

What is a milieu? It is a setting or a situation, the 'set up' in which a dramatic narrative finds itself. This 'set up' might concern the search for a criminal who has committed a crime, it might involve a character's search for true love (as in a romantic narrative), or it might consist of a character's being crossed, and therefore the narrative will constitute a quest for revenge or a settling of scores – and there are any number of types of narrative through which the 'large form' might go. But these are 'big stories' – grand narratives – where there is invariably a beginning, middle and end (and usually in that order as well).

The milieu in John Ford's magnificent film, *Stagecoach* (1939), is constituted first of all by the stagecoach itself. In that coach, seven characters of varying backgrounds are brought together and these backgrounds and characters also contribute to what can be called the milieu: there is the young, well dressed, pregnant lady, Lucy Mallory; there is Dallas the prostitute; the almost permanently inebriated doctor, Doc Boone; the fussy bourgeois salesman, Peacock; the crooked banker, Gatewood; and Hatfield, the suspicious but noble gambling southerner. Along the way they pick up the notorious but good-hearted criminal, Ringo Kid (played by John Wayne). The tensions formed by this group contribute to the milieu: the fact that a gentlewoman must travel side by side with a prostitute; that Ringo Kid must travel as a prisoner; that Gatewood wants to get to the town of Lordsburg without delay; that Lucy's baby is due very soon. And as if that was not enough, the route along which the stagecoach passes is hostile American Indian territory, so perhaps more than anything the milieu is defined by the tension and fear of potential Indian attacks. All of these aspects of the setting and the 'setting up' of the drama constitute the milieu.

If that is the 'milieu' then what are 'modes of behaviour'? There is nothing mysterious in this designation, for 'modes of behaviour' are just that: they are the ways in which people act and the ways in which they are capable of acting. If the milieu is established by the stagecoach and its destination in *Stagecoach*, then 'modes of behaviour' are determined precisely by the ways in which the characters act, by the aims and consequences of their actions. We might consider that the central questions raised by the film are: Will the stagecoach make it to Lordsburg and what actions will the characters need to perform in order to ensure the stagecoach reaches its destination? Supplementary questions follow from these framing ones: Will the conflicts between the characters throw the coach off its course? Will each of the characters discover what they hoped for when they reach their destination? And, perhaps the two questions which lead to the film's climaxes: Will the coach manage to escape an Indian attack (or, if it is attacked, will the passengers be able to defend themselves?); and what will happen to Ringo Kid when he reaches Lordsburg – he has been charged with murder and must face the consequences? Furthermore, Ringo has another motive on his mind: his sworn enemies, the Plummer brothers, are in Lordsburg, so that when he reaches Lordsburg Ringo has but one aim: to kill these brothers. If this constitutes a 'mode of behaviour' (and for Deleuze it certainly does), then we need to ask whether Ringo will be up to the challenge, will he be thrown in jail, or will he be hanged, will he escape, or will he achieve the revenge he desires? In short, *will he be able to act, will his actions be successful?*

Such are the main traits of the 'large form': a milieu in which a situation is defined, and modes of behaviour – the actions – necessary to deal with the situation prescribed by the milieu. We begin to see the ways in which Deleuze's structures fit together, for the milieu works in conjunction with a perception-image, while the modes of behaviour necessitate an action-image. And we can also see how such relations apply to characters and plots: a character perceives something – something wrong, a problem, something that needs to be fixed – and he or she acts on this perception; he or she performs the actions needed to resolve a perceived problem, an action-image responds to a perception-image.

At the same time, at the origin of this perception-action relation is an entire logic of American civilization, according to Deleuze. The large form is nothing if not an 'ethical' image, argues Deleuze. For American cinema, this becomes a matter of distinguishing good from evil:

The ancient or recent past must submit to trial, go to court, in order to disclose what it is that produces decadence and what it is that produces new life . . . . A strong ethical judgement must condemn the injustice of "things", bring compassion, herald the new civilization on the march, in short, constantly rediscover America (Deleuze, 1986, p. 151).

In *Stagecoach* the old, European manners and chivalry (Lucy and Hatfield) must give way to a discovery of the modern virtues of sympathy, self-assertion and 'getting the job done' – Dallas and Doc Boone, for example, offer the support and expertise that facilitate the birth of Lucy's child. The banker Gatewood, on the contrary, is revealed as a criminal, while Ringo – as in a thousand Westerns – demonstrates a mode of ethical behaviour above and beyond the law: his extra-legal vengeance is more satisfactory than the law itself, and his actions herald the emergence of a new civilization as he rides off to his ranch with Dallas, happily ever after.

The law, its shortcomings and its reinvention, is one of the mainstays of Ford's discourses. *Young Mr. Lincoln* (1939), for example, winds its way through a series of conflicts between 'one and the other' – from the pie contest, to the bickering yeomen who squabble over debts, up to the necessity of having to choose between the two brothers in the murder trial. In this film, a higher justice ('Nature') comes to the rescue for Lincoln and a true ethics of a new America emerges along with him (on these points, see the Editors of *Cahiers du cinéma*, 1976). The claims of vengeance (*The Searchers* [1956]) and the problems of dealing with vengeance (*The Man Who Shot Liberty Valance* [1962]) are vital for Ford's Westerns, and the consequences of choosing one path over another – of defending the path of truth, of discovering a true law – are laid bare in a final determinant of the 'large form': the duel. The battle between good and evil, between the true and the false, is typically determined in the large form by a duel or series of duels, where good must confront the evil which has prevented the spread and advance of civilization.

Perhaps nowhere does this occur more enigmatically in Ford's Westerns than in his 1960 film, *Sergeant Rutledge*. This film is a legal drama (like *Lincoln* in this) set in a mythical West of 1881 in which the old institutions of propriety and military nobility – an assumed order of things – are pitted against the new world logics of fairness and truth. Here, then, the milieu is defined by a military court martial in which a Negro sergeant – Rutledge – stands accused of the rape and murder of a young girl as well as the murder of her father, the latter being Rutledge's superior and a distinguished army general. The action is twofold: first, how does Rutledge manage to discover the way to a fair trial? That is, how does he avoid the 'old ways' in which a Negro caught on the wrong side of the law would be summarily lynched by the dominant order of whites, most of whom would presume his guilt and demand execution? The secondary hero of the film is the defence counsel, Tom Cantrell (Jeffrey Hunter, as if returned from his role as Martin Pawley in *The Searchers*, this time as the recognized prophet of truth) who must uncover the truth – of Rutledge's innocence – and ensure the triumph of good over evil and bring into being the ethical founding of a future union. The film's central duel is therefore between the prosecution and the defence, between the traditions of white racial superiority and the dreamed-of destiny of racial justice. The film's denouement is decisive: the white population must pay for the sins they have for so long attributed to the Negro. Only then can America be rediscovered.

Kazan and the American Dream

Elia Kazan raises the four aspects of the large form – the milieu, modes of behaviour, the duel and an ethics in which good triumphs over evil – to a level unprecedented in American cinema. There is an overdetermining anxiety in Kazan's films which centres on trying to ever more clearly define the American dream; that is, of determining the true path towards a reformed civilization and the right modes of action which can bring about such a civilization. The optimism of such an outlook is expressed evocatively in *On the Waterfront* (1954), where the milieu is defined by the corrupt practices of the mob of gangsters who control the labour practices of the New Jersey waterfront workers, and where, in response to the milieu, Terry Malloy (Marlon Brando) employs the modes of behaviour which will alter the milieu and render it 'clean', free from corruption. Malloy 'tells the truth' – there is an ethics of this image in which the truth is rendered pure – and triumphs in the final duel with the mob boss Johnny Friendly: even though he loses the fist fight, he obtains the moral victory, the waterfront in cleansed, and the American dream rediscovered. The fact that all of this occurs in a film in the shadow of Kazan's confessions to the House Un-American Activities Committee only serves to show how difficult the path to the American dream is.

The 'large form' can also be defined by the narrative movement of what Deleuze calls situation-action-situation, or SAS'. The latter situation, designated by S', indicates that an initial situation has changed or been modified. That is to say, if a film puts forward an initial situation, S (the corruption of the waterfront in *On the Waterfront*, for example), then certain actions will need to be performed, A (Malloy will testify against the mob), in order to change or offer a solution to the initial situation. The result will be a new situation, S', typically one in which good has triumphed over evil (the waterfront workers are now free to work without the intimidation of the gangsters), where the true wins out over the false. This designation is one which, Deleuze argues, unfolds according to the laws of 'organic representation', representations where, like those initiated by Griffith, everything will ultimately fit together and find its place: 'organic representation', writes Deleuze, 'is ruled by this last law of development: *there must be a gap between the situation and the action to come, but this gap only exists to be filled*' (Deleuze, 1986, p. 155). Once the gap between an initial situation (S) and the action (A) is filled, a new situation (S') is achieved, and the American dream is rediscovered.

Kazan's *East of Eden* (1955) is exemplary here: a situation (S) in which Cal Trask (James Dean) initially seeks out his presumed long dead mother, while also trying to prove his worth to himself and his father, a father who has for many years failed to understand and appreciate him. Cal therefore acts (A) to bring about a change of this situation, to 'fill the gap' between the situation as it now stands and the 'action to come' which will fill this gap. Cal's father fails in an ambitious business venture, so Cal sets out to win back his father's lost money in the hope therefore of gaining both his admiration and his love. Cal makes back the money, but is still rejected by his father. It is here that we begin to see the other dimension of Kazan's films: the despair at how difficult the American dream is and of how cruelly it can fail. The bitterness and division, the sickness at the heart of

East of Eden seems impossible to overcome, as though the dream has run out, run its course, and America itself is exhausted. And yet, even then, in the depths of despair, Kazan finds hope: at the end of the film, when the father seems to be on his deathbed, he forgives and is miraculously reconciled with Cal. Finally, the action has paid off, the father now understands his son's devotion, he forgives the son his sins, and the dream of a rediscovered America is born again. The modified situation (S') has finally been reached. Deleuze's point in focusing on Kazan is apt: it is when the American dream begins to go sour, when all seems lost, that reinforcing the depth and strength of that dream becomes most crucial:

> The American dream is affirmed more and more to be a dream, nothing other than a dream, contradicted by the facts; but it draws from this a sudden burst of increased power since it now encompasses actions such as betrayal and calumny (the very ones that the dream had the purpose of excluding according to Ford). And it is precisely after the war – at the very moment when the American dream is collapsing, and when the action-image is entering a definitive crisis, as we will see – that the dream finds its most fertile form, and action its most violent, detonating schema. This is the final agony of the action cinema, even if films of this type go on being made for a long time yet (Deleuze, 1986, p. 158)

Marlon Brando, James Dean, Montgomery Clift: these are 'actor's actors', and Kazan, of course, is well-remembered for nurturing the talents of the Actors Studio. In this way, Kazan makes the actions of his characters into 'interior' actions. No longer will America be saved by the actions of a masterful and agile hero who achieves the victory of good over evil as a consequence of bodily strength (or by his 'wits'). Rather, with Kazan, a victory of good becomes an internal struggle, a battle of hearts and minds which the Actors Studio furnishes perfectly. Again and again it is this internal struggle – a struggle for the soul of America – with which Kazan's films engage, from *Gentleman's Agreement* (1947), through *A Streetcar Named Desire* (1951) and *Viva Zapata!* (1952), up to the brilliant later films, *America America* (1963) and *Wild River* (1960), where the battle for America is also a battle for any individual's soul. *Wild River* is perhaps exemplary as it explores the great American experiment of the twentieth century: the New Deal. Kazan's film gently charts the passing of one way of life – the old South, the sternly independent landholder, the accepted denigration of Negroes – as another historical era tries to replace it with equality, fecundity and an embrace of modern 'progress'. The three central characters – Chuck Glover (Montgomery Clift), the grandmother (Jo Van Fleet) and her granddaughter (Lee Remick) – must struggle with each other and with the other townspeople near the Tennessee River, but more than anything they must struggle with themselves. The film's quest is one of independence and self-knowledge, and Chuck indeed tries to instill such enlightenment among the Negro workers.

To Kazan's credit, he proposes in *Wild River* to declare that these means of progress are not simply 'good' while the accepted ways of the South are automatically 'evil'. The film acknowledges that the gains made come at the cost of ruining lives, that battles have both winners and losers, and that the losers often do not deserve their fate. The grandmother's death at the end of the film is a kind of acceptance that there is no longer a place in the world for the likes of her. In contrast to the films of Ford, in which America still awaits its discovery or rediscovery (Ford's films are ones of 'founding'), Kazan presents us with an America which seems to know what it wants, while the people and characters at the mercy of that American vision try to find their place in it, try to work out what they are supposed to do with that vision, and try to work out whether they have any place in it at all. In this way, Kazan presents the ongoing rediscovery of an already founded and civilized America.

The situation-action-modified situation (SAS') form remains for Kazan, even in the later films. In *Wild River*, the grandmother and her homestead must be relocated to allow for the flooding of the Tennessee River. Chuck Glover is sent by the government to persuade the grandmother to leave and, in doing so, he falls in love with the granddaughter. If that is the situation, then the action is that of having the grandmother, her family and the workers at her homestead removed from the land. But we can hardly see that as the film's true action. As I have already claimed, the action that matters is an internal one. Glover, initially full of confidence and bravado, is chastened and at times humiliated and weakened. His own struggle is the quintessential American one: how do I convince others that what I know and what I have idealized is the right way (the good, the true), especially when I come up against another version of what is known and idealized (the good, the true) which so contradicts my own ideality? Glover's 'mode of behaviour' is therefore less of 'getting the job done' than of reconciling himself to what he is doing and what will be done. *His* America is not *all* America. He might be able to persuade the granddaughter to come with him (and they marry, thus preserving the dream that some will manage to take the leap from the old ways to the New Deal), but he knows his actions will also consign a certain version of America to history. And it was Kazan's own struggles with what he wanted to achieve for America, and what America might be able to achieve for him, that makes those films at once so inspiring and at the same time so despicable. His films show us the triumph of American cinema and the action-image.

4

The Movement-Image (III): Hawks and Hitchcock

The Small Form of the Action-Image: Howard Hawks

If the large form of the action-image delivers the triumph of American cinema, then what does Deleuze mean by the 'small form of the action-image'? For Deleuze, if the large form follows the form SAS', then the small form reverses this: its form is ASA'. It is not a complete reversal, however, for the small form is not as rounded and totalizing as the large form. Instead of being contained by an ethical imperative and the duel form in which good struggles against evil (as we saw with the large form), the small form can jump almost endlessly from one action to another action, and another and so on. A typical small form film will begin in the middle of an action with no specific goal or intention being immediately evident. Only once an initial action is completed will a situation then reveal itself. But such a situation will usually only be temporary and will soon be replaced by another action which, in leaps and bounds and by circuitous paths, leads the film's story forward.

Howard Hawks's rambling Western, *The Big Sky* (1952), begins with Jim Deakins (Kirk Douglas) on horseback trotting through some thick forested undergrowth in search of a pig he is hunting. When he accidentally falls, he lands beside a poisonous snake that seems ready to bite him. In the nick of time he is saved by the knife of another man, Boone Caudill. They exchange banter (and one or two punches) before deciding to head off together in the direction of St Louis. The initial action of Jim's confrontation with the snake (A) therefore establishes a situation in which these two men are brought together (S). At this point, however, no central plot or aim or goal is established. Rather, these men's situation of being brought together and forming a friendship establishes an important strand of the story which will follow, but it can hardly be said to be a centralizing or motivating plot element (at any rate, it cannot be said to be such a thing at this stage of the film). In other words, films like this – those of the small form of the action-image – move from one action to another, actions which land their protagonists in one situation, then another, and another and so on.

We can usefully contrast the opening of *The Big Sky* with the beginning of Ford's *Stagecoach*. In the latter, the seven protagonists enter the coach, and this establishes the film's situation (S). That is, it establishes the characters and also the relations between them so that *Stagecoach*'s opening scenes serve to set in place the situation which it will take the rest of the film to sort out. If this, then, is a large form, then it is so because it will take the course of the entire film to bring about the solutions to the problems set out in the initial situation. The problems and solutions of a film like *The Big Sky* are, on the contrary, small ones: the problems pop up, as though out of nowhere, they demand quick solutions (that is, they require actions), and when one action solves a problem, one can be sure there will soon be another problem, most likely around the next corner or bend in the river.

The protagonists in *The Big Sky* stumble from one action to another and from one situation to another. Boone's search for his uncle, Zeb Calloway, takes him and Deakins to St Louis, where they promptly start drinking and singing ('Oh whisky leave me alone') and fighting – all of which we may consider *actions* – which promptly lands them both in jail, thus providing a new *situation*. We can therefore see here how an action necessarily leads to a new situation in films of the small form. In the jail, Boone and Deakins discover none other than Boone's uncle Zeb and, after paying a fine, the three of them decide to join a party of traders who are embarking on a trip up the Missouri River (a new *action*). And such is the course the film takes: one action puts the characters in a new situation, which then leads to new actions and thus to other new situations.

Deleuze claims that much of the action that unfolds in films of the small form arises from the consequences of an *index*. The late nineteenth century American philosopher, Charles Sanders Peirce (1839–1914), upon whose ideas Deleuze relies heavily in *Cinema 1* (ideas on which we can touch only very briefly in the present book), famously distinguished three types of signs: the icon, the symbol and the index. An icon is a sign which resembles that of which it is a sign; a symbol is the kind of sign which is related to its signifier only by virtue of a symbolic connection; while an index is a sign which is in some way intrinsically related to the object of which it is a sign. Classic indices are smoke, for smoke is a sign of fire which is intrinsically connected to the fire of which it is a sign ('where there's smoke, there's fire') and the pointing of a finger (the 'index' finger), which points at the 'there it is' of a thing.

In the small form of the action-image, Deleuze distinguishes two types of index. First of all, there is the *index of lack*. The index of lack implies that something is missing, that there is a 'hole in the story', a situation which is not revealed and which must be discovered (Deleuze, 1986, p. 160). At one point in *The Big Sky*, the party of traders is attacked by Indians and, as a result, Jim Deakins is shot in the leg. Upon removing the bullet, Deakins notices some strange markings on it. What do these markings mean? We can see these markings as evidence of an index of lack – the index is an action ('being shot by a bullet') from which an as yet unknown situation must be inferred (see Bogue, 2003, p. 89). The first presumption is that Deakins has been shot by hostile Indians from the Crow tribe. Later, however, when they confront some members of a rival fur trading company, a company which is trying to monopolize fur trade along the Missouri, they discover that these rivals have bullets with the same strange markings on them. Thus, Deakins works out that he was not shot by the Crow Indians but by these rival fur traders. And yet, this discovery further advances our protagonists' understanding of the situation, for they realize that it was the rival traders who had encouraged the Crow Indians to attack, for the Crow had been a peaceful tribe for many years prior to this attack. From an initial point at which an index (*the bullet*) opened up a hole in the story (*who fired this bullet?*), we now have the information to fill this hole: the rival fur company is trying to sabotage the group's mission on the Missouri River. This, therefore, is one way in which the plot of a small form film will unfold, by way of *indices of lack*.

The other type of index identified by Deleuze is the *index of equivocity*. We shall investigate how this arises in one of Hawks's other great films, *Gentlemen Prefer Blondes* (1953). First of all, this film follows the classic small form: the action of the film begins as the two main characters, Lorelei Lee (Marilyn Monroe) and Dorothy Shaw (Jane Russell) set off on a luxury ocean liner heading for France. The reason they are doing this is because Lorelei wants to be married to the wealthy Gus Esmond (Tommy Noonan), and Gus knows his father will not approve of the marriage, so he has planned to run off to France and be married away from his father's prohibitions. Gus is not sailing with the girls, however, and he plans to meet up with them in France after they have arrived there.

Along the way a number of what Deleuze would call *indices of equivocity* are revealed. First of all, there is Monroe/Lorelei's face: its wide-eyed blankness and seductiveness is dazzlingly impenetrable. This first index of equivocity asks: does Lorelei love Gus or is she merely after him for his money? When on the cruise, Lorelei meets Sir Francis Beekman (Charles Coburn) and suddenly falls in love with him, knowing he is the owner of a company which mines diamonds, we are forced to ask the same question: *does she love him or his money?* Meanwhile, while still on the cruise ship, Beekman gives Lorelei an extravagant diamond tiara, even though this tiara seems to belong to Beekman's wife (and Lady Beekman is herself on the cruise ship too). The tiara thus becomes an index of equivocity: is it a sign of Beekman's love (or desire) for Lorelei? Is it a sign that he no longer cares for his wife? And when Lorelei is accused of stealing the tiara, might this latter version of events be closer to the truth; that is, that Lorelei's love of diamonds has gotten the better of her?

Dorothy – the brunette of the pair – becomes enamoured of another man, Ernie Malone, while on the ship. When she discovers him taking covert photographs of Lorelei in a compromising situation with Francis Beekman, she begins to wonder what Malone is all about: is he the 'nice guy' he seems to be, or is that merely a front for a more sinister motive? Is he merely feigning being a nice guy in order to investigate and expose Lorelei? Malone, we might say, functions as an index of equivocity. What Dorothy suspects is that Malone has been hired by Gus Esmond's father to 'keep an eye on' Lorelei while she is on the cruise ship. If Malone can secure evidence against her, then Esmond's father can step in and call off the proposed marriage. So Malone emerges here as himself an index of equivocity. Deleuze specifically defines this second version of the index as follows: 'a very slight difference in the action, or between two actions, leads to a very great distance between two situations' (Deleuze, 1986, p. 162). Does Lorelei love Gus or merely his money? Is the tiara a gift of love or merely a way for Lorelei to secure the riches of diamonds? Is Malone romantically interested in Dorothy or is he merely using her in order to expose Lorelei? In *Gentlemen Prefer Blondes* indices of equivocity are everywhere.

So, what happens next? When the women arrive in Paris, Lorelei is accused of stealing the tiara. Esmond therefore breaks off his credit leaving Dorothy and Lorelei stranded in Paris with no money. They are forced take a job in a burlesque theatre (such had been their occupation in New York). One night, after performing the number 'Diamonds are a Girl's Best Friend' while Gus Esmond is in the audience – he has come to Paris to explain himself to her and break off their relationship for good – Lorelei is arrested for stealing the tiara, and she just has time for one last goodbye to Gus. Alarmingly, she also discovers that the tiara has been stolen from her, so now she does not even have the option of merely returning the object so as to clear her name. Now, at the same time, Malone, who has been shadowing Gus all along – and who thus knows that Lorelei has been arrested and will face a judge at a night court this very night – is at the Paris airport to greet Esmond's father, who has come to Paris to check on his son. Esmond Sr thanks Malone for a job well done – so we now know for certain that Malone has been working for Esmond, thus bringing to an end one of the indices of equivocity. While at the airport, Malone also runs into Francis Beekman, who inadvertently introduces himself as 'Amos Finch' and then excuses himself for apparently having had a bit of a joke.

As a result of this, Malone gets suspicious and he accompanies Mr Esmond Sr to the night court where Lorelei is facing a judge. Now, it is clear as day to viewers of the film and to Malone who the person is who is sitting in the accused's chair – it is not Lorelei, but Dorothy dressed in a blonde wig to imitate Lorelei. Neither Mr Esmond Sr is aware of this (for he has never set eyes on Lorelei before) nor is the prosecuting attorney whose extremely thick glasses clearly betray a poor sense of sight. It is here that the index of equivocity is taken to its extreme: if Lorelei's visage had been equivocal in the past then here it is a different face altogether! By way of a series of pantomimes, the disguised Dorothy declares her love for Malone, while Malone gathers a few gendarmes together to go to the airport to arrest Francis Beekmam who is exposed as a conman – Amos Finch is indeed his name – and who has the stolen tiara in his possession. The tiara's role as an index of equivocity has now run its course: Lorelei did not steal it, but was instead the victim of a conman's plot.

There is, of course, a final question for the resolution of the narrative: does Lorelei really love Gus? The film handles this point quite brilliantly, for, having left the night court, Esmond Sr goes to the club where his son is still 'saying goodbye' to the real Lorelei. When Esmond Sr confronts the couple, he is delighted that Gus has decided to marry this woman, for he is unaware that this woman is, in fact, Lorelei herself. Upon discovering that this woman is supposed to be Lorelei, he exclaims, 'You don't fool me one bit'. Thus ensues the following exchange of banter between them:

Lorelei: I'm not trying to [fool you], but I bet I could . . . But I do love him.
Esmond Sr: Yes, for his money.
L: No, honestly.
E: Have you got the nerve to stand there and tell me you don't want to marry my son for his money?
L: Certainly . . . , I want to marry him for *your* money!
E: You admit that all you're after is money, aren't you?
L: No (she smiles). Aren't you funny? Don't you know that a man being rich is like a girl being pretty? You might not marry a girl just because she's pretty, but my goodness doesn't it help? And if you had a daughter, wouldn't you rather she didn't marry a poor man? You'd want her to have the most wonderful things in the world and to be very happy. Well, why is it wrong for me to want those things?

And that's just about enough to convince the father that the marriage is a good match. It closes the final index of equivocity: does Lorelei really love Gus, or does she only love him for his money? And the answer is: both!

There are myriad examples of the small form which Deleuze discusses in *Cinema 1*. It applies forcefully, for Deleuze, to the films of Buster Keaton and Charlie Chaplin, and to the Westerns of Anthony Mann. It also opens onto an important mode for Eisenstein's films, for Deleuze argues that Eisenstein's films primarily trace a course that begins with the promptings of the large form, but finally ends up in something that resembles the small form. We cannot chart the details of these moves made by the small form here, but we must emphasize one more key point Deleuze makes: if the grand actions of the large form were ones which promised the founding of a new society and the moral victory of good over evil, then the small form of the action-image contains very little of such promises. As Deleuze puts it: 'Nothing is ever won . . . . For there is no longer any grandiose action at all, even if the hero has retained extraordinary technical qualities' (Deleuze, 1986, p. 168). Jim Deakins might display extraordinary skill in helping the boat find its way up the Missouri River against tremendous odds. Lorelei Lee and Dorothy Shaw are skilful in their own ways too: they scheme, trick, dance and sing their ways out of trouble and score husbands into the bargain. But none of these heroes has saved the world or founded a new civilization; they have not even ensured the victory of good over evil. Rather, they have 'gotten by', they have 'made do', with whatever goods and by whatever means were necessary. As Deleuze argues of the heroes of the small form, 'They have kept nothing of the American dream, they have only kept their lives' (Deleuze, 1986, p. 168).

The Relation-Image: Alfred Hitchcock

For Deleuze, Alfred Hitchcock perfects something that the action cinema had tended to overlook: the third term. If both the large and the small forms are based on binary couplings – the duel structure of the large form and the AS momentum of the small form – then Hitchcock's films introduce a third term. Again relying on Peirce's philosophies of signification and logic (see Deleuze, 1986, pp. 197–8), Deleuze argues that if the doubled structures of classical American cinema concern the relationship between perception and action, between a perception-image and an action-image, the third term introduces something new: *interpretations* and *mental relations*. And the master of such relations is Hitchcock: 'In Hitchcock, actions, affections, perceptions, all is interpretation, from beginning to end' (ibid., p. 200).

Deleuze outlines five specific traits of what he calls the relation-image in Hitchcock's films:

1   a relational third term

2   an initiating action that opens a web of relations

3   an exchange of crimes

4   a series of *marks* and *demarks*

5   a relation between a film and its spectator

In order to discern what Deleuze means by these designations, it will be necessary to examine them one at a time. In doing so, the focus will be on two of Hitchcock's films: *Strangers on a Train* (1951) and *Vertigo* (1958).

(1) *A relational third term*. To define it most simply, the relational third term is that of *thought*. If classical American cinema was based on relations between perceptions and actions, then the third term Hitchcock introduces is one which has to do with thought, the mental relations which contribute to a film's processes of signification. More specifically, Deleuze focuses on what, in Hitchcock's films, amounts to 'a line of reasoning', the fact that, in Hitchcock's films, characters – as well as the members of the audience – are forced to ask questions and develop interpretations in order to work out what is going on, to puzzle through who might have done what, and what the solution to a character's predicament might be. In *Strangers on a Train*, the 'line of reasoning' follows two paths. First, in the opening sequence on the train in which the tennis player, Guy Haines (Farley

Granger) meets Bruno Antony (Robert Walker), the latter sets up a line of thought: *if I were to kill the wife you no longer love, then you, Guy, could kill my father whom I hate.* We could, Bruno explains, exchange murders. As Guy does not know Bruno – this is the first time they have met – there will be nothing to connect Guy with the murder of Bruno's father, and likewise, there would be nothing to connect Bruno with the murder of Guy's wife; they might just be able to commit the perfect murders! Guy's inadvertent agreement with Bruno's scheme ('Of course I agree – I agree with all your theories') plants the thought which will become a relational third term between Guy and Bruno.

Once Bruno has committed the murder of Guy's wife, Guy becomes the chief suspect, so the line of reasoning now changes to become the kind of thing we might typically expect of a thriller: *how will Guy manage to get himself out of this mess?* But this *is* absolutely central to the film: the conundrum of trying to figure out how Guy can get out of this tricky web that has been spun around him. It is not just a matter of Guy hunting down the killer and exposing him, as we might expect of the large form of the action-image (the solution to a crime). Instead, the third term, the line of reasoning, is intrinsic: Guy must figure out how he can put Bruno in such a position as to reveal him as the killer. (We have here the 'wrong man' scenario beloved of Hitchcock: *Young and Innocent* [1937], *The Wrong Man* [1956], *North by Northwest* [1959].)

(2) *An initiating action that opens a web of relations.* Robin Wood, in his excellent essay on *Strangers on a Train*, points to the importance of the film's opening moments:

> The first shots introduce us to two pairs of men's feet as their owners arrive at a station. The two are characterized by means of their shoes: first, showy, vulgar, brown and white brogues; second, plain, unadorned walking shoes . . . . On the train, we are shown the feet again, moving to the same table. It is always Bruno's feet that we see first – he arrives at the station first, he sits down first; it is Guy's foot that knocks his accidentally, under the table, leading directly to their getting into a conversation (Wood, 2009, p. 172).

Hitchcock is indeed a master of the accidental meeting – or occurrence – George Kaplan (*North by Northwest*), Melanie and Mitch (*The Birds* [1963]), L. B. Jeffries's broken leg (*Rear Window* [1954]) – which sets in motion an unfolding of events, and *Strangers on a Train* is no exception. It is the mere fact of Bruno and Guy's meeting, and the initially unremarkable exchanges of banter between them – 'Aren't you the tennis player Guy Haines?' Bruno asks – that sets in motion a plot that slowly and surely spins out of control.

But what is it that opens up out of this initiating action? Deleuze argues that a typical result in Hitchcock's films is a *web of relations*. In other words, in Hitchcock we cannot usually reduce the plot to a tangle between two characters – a hero and a villain. Rather, even if we do have a hero and a villain, the intricate connections and expanding relations in which our hero and villain are swept up send the plots of these films to the limit of containability. In *Rear Window*, for example, we not only have Jeffries (the hero) and Thorwald (the villain), but we also have Lisa (Jeffries' love interest), the musician, Miss Torso, Miss Lonely Hearts, all of the characters who become entangled in the mystery of the apartment block. In *Psycho* (1960), we not only have Marion (the victim) and Norman Bates (the villain), we also have Marion's love interest, the detective, Norman's mother and so on. None of these are 'bit' characters, for they are essential to the 'web' Hitchcock so carefully weaves in his films; they are essential to the development of the 'line of reasoning' that operates by way of the relational third term – in *Rear Window*, it is the question of *did Thorwald murder his wife* while in *Psycho* it is the question of *who killed Marion?*

(3) *An exchange of crimes. Strangers on a Train* is exemplary in this respect, for here, a central aspect of the plot is an 'exchange of crimes': Bruno's proposal is precisely that he and Guy exchange murders. If a crime of one sort or another is usually central to Hitchcock's films – and it usually is – then these crimes are also usually never straightforwardly committed. Instead, the crime is passed from one character to another, as it is in *Strangers on a Train*, but such a gambit operates in *The Wrong Man*, *North by Northwest*, *The 39 Steps* (1935), *Psycho*, *The Man Who Knew Too Much* (1956), even *Notorious* (1946), *Suspicion* (1941), *Mr and Mrs Smith* (1941),

The Trouble with Harry (1955) and *Rebecca* (1940) can be said to unfold along such lines.

(4) *A series of* marks *and* demarks. Deleuze argues that, in Hitchcock's films, the *mark* is something which establishes a series of relations between things or which places events into some kind of series. The *demark*, on the other hand, is something which upsets the relations and the series set in place by the mark. In *Strangers on a Train* the mark and demark are particularly bold: the cigarette lighter on which is inscribed 'From A to G' forms the most prominent mark, while the glasses Miriam was wearing when she was murdered and which resemble the glasses worn by Ann Morton's younger sister, Barbara, acts as the most prominent demark. (For those unfamiliar with the plot, Ann Morton, a senator's daughter, is the woman Guy intends to marry, but in order to do so, he needs first of all to 'get rid of' his wife, Miriam.)

How do the lighter and the glasses act as the mark and the demark? Guy first offers the lighter to Bruno so that he may light his cigarette, and Bruno is drawn to the inscription 'From A to G'. He surmises, having read about Guy in the newspapers (Haines is a famous tennis player), that the lighter must have been a gift from Ann to Guy and hence, the lighter contributes to the formulation of Bruno's plan for the perfect murder. But we can also suggest that the inscription portends to the exchange between Guy and Bruno, for Bruno's surname is Antony, so that the inscription might come to mean from Antony to Guy, certainly in as much as Bruno gives his crime to Guy. In short, the mark – the lighter – sets in train a 'customary series' (Deleuze, 1986, p. 203) of relations, the relations which refer to the murder of Guy's wife and to the relations between Guy and Bruno, and between Guy and Ann, which are swept up in this series.

The demark signals the point where this series of so-called 'natural' relations established by the mark begins to come unstuck. The two dizzy spells or trances which Bruno falls into when he sets eyes on Barbara's glasses – the reminders or signs of guilt which overwhelm him – are the demarks which eventually, as it were, 'give the game away'. And Hitchcock is certainly famous for these kinds of signs: the crop-dusting airplane in *North by Northwest*, the guilty man's twitch in *Young and Innocent*, the bottles of wine in *Notorious*, the windmill in *Foreign Correspondent* (1940).

And yet, the cigarette lighter itself also changes function: while first of all it functions as a mark of the series which connects Bruno and Guy, it turns out that it is precisely this connection that Bruno must undo if he is to pin the murder on Guy. Or, to put it another way, for as long as it is in Bruno's possession, the cigarette lighter will *mark* him, and the final turn of the plot hinges on Bruno's attempts to make this lighter *demark* him, as it were. This final act will allow Bruno to transfer his crime 'from A (Antony) to G (Guy)'. Again, for those unfamiliar with the plot: Bruno returns to the scene of the crime in order to plant the lighter there, for if a lighter belonging to Guy Haines is found at the murder scene, then surely it will be clear evidence that Guy is guilty and Bruno will be able to go free – such is his plan. All along the way, however, Bruno stumbles and fumbles, and the lighter, as a *demark*, is the sign of the guilt he carries with him: first, when another passenger on the train asks him for a light, he quickly shoves the lighter in his pocket and pulls out some matches instead – he does not want to be seen with *this* lighter! And later, just after he has gotten off the train and is nearing the murder scene, he is knocked by someone passing him and he drops the lighter into a storm drain, and there follows a long sequence in which he tries to retrieve the lighter from the drain. And finally, Bruno's fate is sealed, and Guy's innocence proven, when at the film's climax Bruno is discovered clutching the lighter: the object that had first opened the exchange of crimes (the *mark*) has now proven that the crimes were not exchanged (the *demark*) and Bruno's plot has been foiled.

(5) *A relation between a film and its spectator.* Films – it goes without saying – have always had spectators, but Hitchcock managed the feat of weaving the spectator into his films. For the characters in his films, and also for the audiences of these films, what was at stake was *interpretation*, a *line of reasoning*, so that, for a film like *Rear Window*, we are all keen to see what Jeffries is thinking and how he is compiling his evidence, but *we too* are compiling and weighing up the evidence along with him: *did Thorwald commit the murder?* The problem to be solved is not merely a problem for the hero of the film, it is a problem for us as well, as viewers of the film. It is in this way that Hitchcock makes essential the relation between a film and its spectator.

There is little question that Hitchcock manages to do such a thing quite evocatively in *Strangers on a Train*. We can again follow Robin Wood here, who isolates a key feature of the film's effect. He argues that the character of Barbara makes explicit 'what everybody – including the spectator', writes Wood, 'is ashamed to admit: that it is really an admirable thing from all points of view that Miriam is dead' (Wood, 2009, p. 177). And Wood continues by claiming that 'we, as well as Guy, are implicated in Miriam's murder' in so far as it is a desirable thing (ibid.). Then our murderous desires are indulged and challenged at the Morton's evening dinner party when Bruno, after some playful banter on the theme of desirable murders, plays a game of strangling one of the guests, only to fall into a trance when his gaze falls on Barbara's glasses so that he nearly does strangle this guest. 'The scene', argues Wood, 'is a superb example of the Hitchcock spectator trap' (Wood, 2009, p. 177) with the implication that, on the one hand, we have been encouraged to believe that murder might be an acceptable or even desirable act, only to be caught out by our momentary identification with the murderous Bruno. It is by way of such techniques that, according to Deleuze, Hitchcock manages to structure his films on the basis of three interwoven factors: 'the director, the film and the public which must come into the film' (Deleuze, 1986, p. 202).

On *Vertigo*

All of these factors are at play in Hitchcock's *Vertigo*.

A relational third term: we can identify any number of third terms throughout *Vertigo*. Why is Madeleine behaving in such a strange way? is the question that occupies the first half of the film, for Madeleine seems to be possessed by a figure from the past, Carlotta Valdez. If we therefore understand the key characters of this part of the film as Scottie (James Stewart) and Madeleine (Kim Novak), then Carlotta is the figure who motivates a 'line of reasoning', a 'third term'. But we might also see Scottie as the third term who intervenes in the relationship between Madeleine and her husband, Gavin Elster. Alternatively, we might even see Madeleine as a third term which disrupts the friendship between Scottie and Midge (Barbara Bel Geddes). Whichever way we choose to look at it, there is a whole tangled web of triadic relations in *Vertigo*.

Even then, the second half of the film – following the death of the 'first Madeleine' – introduces a whole new series of third terms. For a start, we come to realize that Judy (the 'second Madeleine') was, during the first half of the film, a third term between Elster and his wife (the 'real' Madeleine). And now, for the second half of the film she becomes a third term for Scottie, for it is Judy who provides a point of connection between Scottie and his memory and longing for Madeleine. It is Judy who provides the possibility of discovering a 'line of reasoning' for what happened to him. Hence Scottie's anguished cries at the end of the film, 'Why did you do it Judy?' Third terms, lines of reasoning and mental relations abound in *Vertigo*. In Hitchcock's films, Deleuze argues, 'There is not only the action and acting, the assassin and the victim, there is always a third and not an accidental or apparent third . . . but a fundamental third constituted by the relation [between the first two terms]' (Deleuze, 1986, p. 201).

The web of relations: the initiating action which opens the web of relations might well be the onset of Scottie's vertigo and his retirement from the police force. However, this initiating action only really takes on momentum in so far as Elster then makes his proposal to Scottie: *please follow my wife in order to find out what is wrong with her.* Elster's asking Scottie for a 'favour', and Scottie's acceptance of that task is *Vertigo*'s definitive initiating action. It sets in train a web of relations from which Scottie finds it impossible to escape.

The exchange of crimes: Elster exchanges his crime with Scottie – for Elster is clearly the guilty party here while Scottie is the one who pays the price. It is Scottie, for example, who has to endure the brutal examination at the investigation into the death of the 'first Madeleine', and it is he who suffers a nervous breakdown. However, we can also suggest that Judy exchanges her crime with the first Madeleine: Judy's crime of imitating Madeleine is extinguished when the first Madeleine is killed, and thus the crime is given to the first Madeleine and dies with her. Of course, later, Judy's crime catches up with Scottie, and we would have to conclude that, in the end, it is Scottie who is the eventual recipient of both Elster's crime (the murder of Madeleine) and Judy's deceitful act as accomplice.

A series of marks and demarks: in Vertigo, the mark emerges as a result of the series of relations established between Carlotta and Madeleine. This necessitates the series of events whereby Madeleine travels to the florist, the art gallery at the Palace of the Foreign Legion, San Francisco bay, Carlotta's grave, McKittrick's hotel; all of these are set into play by the Madeleine-Carlotta dyad. The demark, on the other hand, is a factor which throws the series off track; the demark completely upsets the series set in place by the mark. Judy is no doubt the demark in Vertigo, for her arrival completely undermines everything that had been established by the mark, to the point where everything to do with the series set up by the mark is revealed to be a sham. After the death of Madeleine, the Carlotta-Madeleine mark still has a hold, as Scottie searches the landmarks that are 'marked' as it were: Carlotta's grave, the art gallery, Ernie's restaurant, the flower store. Only when Judy writes her letter to Scottie (which is never sent), and effectively exposes to the audience the nature of the ruse she had conducted with Elster, is the mark disrupted by the demark: the whole film changes after this pivotal scene. To take another example: in Psycho, the mark established by the illicit affair between Sam and Marion establishes a series leading to Marion's stealing of the $40,000, her fleeing town, her buying a new car, her stopping at the Bates Motel, while this all changes via Norman Bates's function as the demark (or, strictly speaking, his murder of Marion), which sets the film onto a different course.

A relation between a film and its spectator: Vertigo's mark and demark are the provocations by which the spectator is made essential to the film. It is not merely Scottie who tries to determine a line of reasoning out of Madeleine's obsession with Carlotta, but the spectator too must ask after some sort of reasoning as a process of watching the film: why is Madeleine 're-living' Carlotta's life? Why does she fall into San Francisco bay? What is the significance of the Spanish mission? These are all questions to which Scottie tries to find answers in the first half of the film, but we, as spectators, also try to determine the answers to these questions, a questioning that is especially effective when Scottie is closely following Madeleine in the early scenes of the film. The public, thus, comes into the film.

The spectator's inclusion in the second half of the film is even more significant. Hitchcock himself stated the significance of revealing Judy's story to the audience while concealing it from Scottie. As mentioned earlier, by way of a letter she intends to send to Scottie, but does not, Judy explains the way that Elster had made her into Madeleine, and that Scottie was the 'real victim' of Elster's scheme. Hitchcock was adamant that, for *Vertigo* to achieve its appropriate effect, the audience must know more than Scottie (of course, it is a technique of his to grant the audience more knowledge than characters – a technique fundamental for suspense). In an often quoted anecdote he explains:

> Though Stewart [that is, Scottie] isn't aware of it yet, the viewers know that Judy isn't just a girl who looks like Madeleine, but that she *is* Madeleine! Everyone around me was against this change; they all felt that the revelation should be saved for the end of the picture. I put myself in the place of a child whose mother is telling him a story. When there's a pause in her narration, the child always says, 'What comes next, Mommy?' Well, I felt that the second part of the novel was written as if nothing came next, whereas in my formula, the little boy, *knowing* that Madeleine and Judy are the same person, would then ask, 'And Stewart doesn't know it, does he? What will he do when he finds out about it?'[1]

Hitchcock puts himself in the place of the audience, and furthermore into the position of a child, but importantly, he charts here the essential nature of the audience in the unfolding of *Vertigo*'s narrative. The interruption of the demark – the introduction of the character of Judy – allows a new line of reasoning to emerge for the film. When Scottie finds Judy, she becomes the key to making him happy once again (the few days he spends with her he regards as 'the happiest in a year'). But Judy can only make him happy because she provides the possibility of his re-finding his lost love, of re-finding Madeleine. He believes his only cure will be to re-find the object of his desire, hence his quest to remake Judy into Madeleine by way of which his illness may be cured. If this is Scottie's quest, then the audience now has a different question, because we, the viewers, already know that Judy *is* Madeleine. Our question, as Hitchcock points out, is 'what will Scottie do when he finds out?' Again, the audience is central to Hitchcock's conception of *Vertigo*.

5

The Time-Image (I): Italian Neorealism and After

What is the Time-Image?

In the history of cinema there is, for Deleuze, something that can be called a movement-image, but alongside this – (or in opposition to it? Or after it? Or beyond it? These are questions that might be difficult to answer) – he also discovers something called a time-image. As noted in Chapter 1 of this book, for films of the movement-image, time is subordinated to movement, while films of the time-image, argues Deleuze, present 'a little time in the pure state', a 'direct-image of time' (see Deleuze, 1989, p. 169). Such phrases do not immediately clarify what a time-image might be. There are, however, two key factors which primarily define what is meant by the time-image. First of all, the time-image creates a relation between the past, the present and the future which is somewhat different to that presented by the movement-image. Films of the movement-image, Deleuze argues, assert a perspective on the past which is at the mercy of the present. He writes that such films have the function of *making the present past* (Deleuze, 1989, p. 35), of clarifying the existence of the present by clarifying the past and, therefore, of putting the present in a relation to the past that puts both on a firm footing. If the movement-image strives for clarity in this respect – that is, to clearly separate the present from the past – then films of the time-image throw such clarity into question. Deleuze evocatively states that, for the time-image, 'there is no present which is not haunted by a past and future' (ibid., p. 38). Unlike what is expected of the movement-image, the task of the time-image is not one of assuring us that the present is *here* and the past *there*. Rather, the task for films of the time-image is to declare that if the present is *here*, then the past is here with it, and so too is the future. And if the present is discovered to be *there* (and not *here*), then so too may the past and the future be *there*, but they may also be *here*. They might even be both here and there. This openness of time – of a time that is not locked into a certain past and a clarified present – is what Deleuze means by a *direct image of time*. 'It is characteristic of cinema', he writes, 'to seize this past and this future that coexist with the present image' (ibid., p. 37).

The second key factor by which the time-image can be defined is that characters in these films have difficulty finding solutions to problems. If films of the movement-image, as I have claimed previously, can be defined by their quests to solve problems, and by the success of such quests, then films of the time-image are not defined in such a way. There are still problems in these films which seem to require solutions, and there are even characters who seek to find solutions to those problems. But it is rare that they find solutions, and if they do, these solutions will fail to be definitive or universal. Rather, if there are problems to be solved then characters in films of the time-image typically come to realize that they are problems which cannot be easily solved: no final duel or showdown will suffice to rid the world of evil and establish the bounds of a newly cleansed civilization. Instead, the characters in these films come to understand that the kinds of problems they confront are not ones that can be easily solved (and we have seen as much in our discussion of Hitchcock's *Vertigo*, a film very much on the border between movement-image and time-image). They are problems which lead characters to being frozen, confused, disappointed, fractured and alienated, but also to their being reborn, rejuvenated and strengthened.

Consider the most famous film of Italian neorealism, *Bicycle Thieves* (1948). We might initially think this film is organized around the quest to solve a problem: for Antonio to discover who stole his bicycle and, by way of a final duel, to win back his bicycle and thus to live happily ever after. From such a perspective, good will win over evil and a civilization of good can be established over the barbarity of evil. And yet, in *Bicycle Thieves*, this is not what occurs. Antonio does not solve the problem of who stole his bicycle and nor does he therefore capture the thief and punish the wrongdoer. Instead, he discovers something else: he realizes that recovering his bicycle will not solve his problems or the problems of the society that surround him. By the end of the film he is at a loss to know what to do, his actions have amounted to nothing – his appeals to the police, the Church and the labour union are in vain, his attempts to capture a man whom he thinks is the thief merely ends in his own humiliation, and his attempt to steal another person's bicycle also backfires. In this film, a film of the time-image, Antionio's actions no longer have the kinds of consequences they would once have had for films of the movement-image.

With *Bicycle Thieves* in mind we can consider how the time-image emerges out of the crisis of the movement-image. As we have seen, with filmmakers like Howard Hawks and Alfred Hitchcock, the movement-image is taken to its limit. In contrast with the large form of the action-image, Hawks's small form films retain little of the American dream. The heroes of these films do not save the world, they do not assert an ethical form of good over evil; they merely manage to save their own lives. Here, the grandeur and ambition of the movement-image have begun to fade. Hitchcock then pushes the movement-image beyond action so that interpretation or thought – 'mental relations' – becomes central to the image. In Hitchcock, the action-image is eclipsed in favour of mental relations, and the solution to problems is no longer a task to be performed but a problem to be solved by virtue of a relation-image. Beyond Hitchcock and beyond the movement-image, the time-image emerges when the problem can no longer be solved. We are left only with thought, of thoughts that are yet to be thought (for the solution to the problem is yet to be discovered) and an evocation of 'a little time in the pure state'.

But why is this image of thought yet to be thought somehow an image of 'time'? The movement-image, as stated previously, effectively fixes the past and the future in place – its aim is to ensure the fixity of relations between past, present and future. In other words, the aim of the films of the movement-image is to find out what *really* happened in the past so that we can then understand the present and, finally, know what to do in the future. Such things occur in the films we have examined: in *On the Waterfront*, Terry Malloy discovers that he could have and should have been a contender, and this new perspective on his past sets him on a determined course for his future; in *Wild River* the future is set on course as a way of overcoming the inadequacies of the past (that is, the continued flooding of the Tennessee Valley); in *Stagecoach*, the Ringo Kid lays to rest the disturbances of his past, he 'settles the score' with the Plummer brothers and paves the way for a future; *Sergeant Rutledge* is concerned with clarifying the past (who killed the young girl and her father?) so as to secure a true future. The fixing of the past will ensure the stability of the present (and its truth) – for we can be certain of 'how the present came to be' – and thus a future can also be fixed: we know what kind of a future beckons because we know the truth of the past and the present (the hope is that, in knowing such things, we will all live 'happily ever after').

In stark contrast with the movement-image, the time-image denies the fixed nature of past, present and future. Its guiding motto might be *rediscover the past*. But even this might not be enough, for films of the time-image rediscover the past *as new*; they engage with the past not in order to know a definitive 'truth' of the past, but instead engage with the past as a territory of discovery. At one point, Deleuze invokes the work of Charles Péguy (1873–1914) who, in his *Clio*, makes a distinction between trying to discover *what really happened in the past* by gathering the relevant facts and evidence, and, on the contrary, an encounter with the past that involves *going back into the past* as though one were taking one's place in it, swimming in it (see Deleuze, 1995, pp. 170–1). It is this latter relation to the past, a kind of renewal – a constant renewing – of the past that the time-image seeks. This renewal of the past is simultaneously a rediscovery of the present: a new present born out of a newly discovered past. And, if one discovers that the past was *not like that*, that it does not need to be like that, and that this past will change again the next time it is visited, then one can also imagine a future that is uncharted, that is changeable, uncertain and potentially full of new discoveries. Marcel Proust might be a key figure here, for his *mémoire involuntaire* is precisely what is at stake: a memory from the past which appears as though out of nowhere, and not by conscious provocation, and which strikes one precisely as something long forgotten, as though remembered and experienced here for the first time.

Italian Neorealism

Bicycle Thieves has already been mentioned, but there are many reasons why Deleuze positions Italian neorealism as a crucial moment for the development of the time-image. Neorealism emerges from the rubble of World War II when the rules of one generation (of Mussolini and fascism) are to be replaced by another (a hoped-for democracy). The past and the future are no longer determined by a repressive regime. Instead, the future attains a new openness. Here, Deleuze seems to take Italy as emblematic for the future of the world as such: one era of history has passed, and the end of World War II signals the potential birth of a new era.

And the neorealist filmmakers begin to tell different kinds of stories, ones not based on certainties and grand narratives – there are no 'large form' narratives here – and these filmmakers also introduce different kinds of heroes, ones whose aims are no longer those of founding a new civilization by overcoming evil, but whose destiny is instead merely *to see* (and ultimately to hear, to sense and to think). Deleuze isolates a seemingly innocuous moment from Rossellini's *Europa '51* (1952) as central to his explication of the neorealist breakthrough. Midway through the film, a middle-class woman, Irene (Ingrid Bergman) stops to look at a factory. A reverse shot reveals to us that she looks anxious and perplexed. Later in the film she declares that, when she stopped to look at the factory it seemed to her to look like a prison. Deleuze concludes from this that the factory, as a seemingly singular object, passes through different circuits: at one point it might indeed look like a prison; at another, it will simply look like a factory. Paola Marrati provides an excellent explanation of what is at stake for Deleuze here:

> The woman who no longer 'recognizes' a factory nonetheless sees it; she can see it all the better because she does not 'recognize' it. Learning to see, or in any case making seeing the central experience, is, for Deleuze, the distinctive discovery of neorealism (Marrati, 2008, p. 58).

This form of seeing is a seeing that is not bound to what one has learned to see or been told to see. It is, we might say, the experience of seeing something as though for the first time so that one is seeing it not on the basis of what one already knows, but instead on the basis of what is unknown. Deleuze calls these experiences or situations *purely optical situations*:

> What defines neo-realism is this build up of purely optical situations . . . which are fundamentally distinct from the sensory-motor situations of the action-image in the old realism (Deleuze, 1989, p. 2).

Neorealism therefore foregrounds purely optical situations rather than presenting the sensory-motor situations typical of the movement-image. What Deleuze means by 'sensory-motor' are simply those actions and activities of the body, those performances of action which lead to the solution of problems – such as that exhibited by the Ringo Kid in *Stagecoach*, or by the eviction of the grandmother in *Wild River*, or even of those actions which secure marriage for the women in *Gentlemen Prefer Blondes*. By contrast, films of the time-image – such as *Europa '51* – feature blockages of sensory-motor ability; that is, characters cease to have the ability to perform the actions necessary to solve a problem. Instead, the characters in these films 'learn to see': their senses are revivified and the world for them is seen in a new light. 'To see the world anew' might be the central task of the time-image. 'This is a cinema of the seer', claims Deleuze, 'and no longer of the agent' (Deleuze, 1989, p. 2).

Irene, the heroine of *Europa '51*, is an exemplar of the kind of character who learns to see the world differently. Following the tragic death of her son, for which she blames herself, Irene begins to devote her life to the poor and neglected in a manner not dissimilar to the St Francis of Rossellini's *Francesco* (1950), made the year before. But her interest in these fringe dwellers – workers, prostitutes and those normally excluded from middle-class concerns – makes her appear entirely abnormal to her family and friends. In the end she is committed to a psychiatric institution, her devotion to those less fortunate than herself being considered so abnormal as to necessitate her exclusion from society. She has broken away from society as it is; she has broken away from the learned routines and ways of looking at the world so as to be able to see that world anew. This ability is what is at stake for the time-image.

Deleuze begins *Cinema 2* with an account of the maid's sequence from *Umberto D* (1952) which impressed André Bazin (see Bazin, 1971a; 1971b). Where Bazin tried to emphasize this scene's realism, Deleuze instead focuses on the way it replaces a cinema of action with a cinema of the senses. In films of the movement-image, actions are foregrounded in order that those actions might produce results and lead to something (a 'conclusion', as it were). But here, in this scene from *Umberto D*, the maid performs a series of actions – grinding the coffee beans, washing the ants away from the sink, pushing the door closed with her outstretched foot – not for the purposes of achieving a result, but rather because . . . . because why? For Deleuze, these actions no longer have the status of actions but are instead *gestures* or *depictions of situations*: 'And her eyes meet her pregnant belly', he writes, so that 'what has been brought about is a *pure optical situation* to which the little maid has no response or reaction. The eyes, the belly, that is what an encounter is . . . ' (Deleuze, 1989, pp. 1–2). This is a cinema where actions and reactions are no longer necessary or even possible. What is encountered here is instead a moment of 'pure seeing' (see Bogue 2003, p. 109).

Antonioni

Why would cinema want to do such things? Why would one want to see subjects who seem to have lost their abilities to function 'properly' (as occurs with Irene in *Europa '51*) or who are caught up in dire straits (as the maid from *Umberto D* is)? Perhaps these questions can be best answered with reference to one of the Italian auteurs who most successfully inherited the problems and questions of Italian neorealism: Michelangelo Antonioni. At the beginning of *Cinema 2*, Antonioni is placed as a successor to the innovations of Italian neorealism. This is especially the case in so far as Antonioni extends the significance of the 'pure optical and sound situations' discovered by the neorealists. He emphasizes the states of dislocation and disintegration experienced by specific characters. For Deleuze, Antonioni reaches the point of *dehumanizing* the situations in which his characters are placed, he presents empty, barren spaces into which the humans themselves seem to have disappeared or been absorbed. The human beings in Antonioni's films disappear into, or are absorbed by, the empty spaces which come to dominate them. Preliminarily it is accurate to declare that something like this happens in the films made by Antonioni on which we will focus here: *L'avventura* (1960), *La Notte* (1961), *L'eclisse* (1962) and *Blow Up* (1966). But a more pressing concern is the question of why the films do this. Why is it significant or important? What is the significance of this emptiness, of this disappearance of the traits of humanness?

One of the key issues Deleuze points towards is that we never get to know Antonioni's characters *from the inside*. Instead, we only get to see them in parallel with other objects of the landscape: buildings, streets, the stock exchange, a nuclear power station, a container ship, motor cars, trains, a house, a pool, a statue and so on. The humans here are composed *as* objects, as though they were merely other objects in a world full of objects. And Deleuze therefore characterizes Antonioni's approach as an *objective* one: he approaches his characters *from the outside*, so that one thing we can say about these characters is that they are not self-willed or self-defined; they are not 'subjects' in the strong sense in which we might understand that term. If they have traits of human subjectivity, then these traits are the ones defined by the other people and objects, the spaces and situations with which they come into contact or which they occupy.

This kind of 'objectification of subjectivity' becomes especially apparent in a small scene from *La Notte*. It happens midway through the film, during the party at the home of the rich industrialist who is a supporter and advocate of the work of Giovanni Pontano (Marcello Mastroianni), a writer who has just published a novel. At this point of the film, we see Giovanni flirting with and eventually kissing the industrialist's daughter, Valentina (Monica Vitti). This might not seem like much until we realize that Giovanni's wife is observing this action: she witnesses the wavering of her husband's faith, a wavering that dominates much of the film. Giovanni's wife, Lidia (Jeanne Moreau), has also, immediately prior to witnessing her husband's flirtation, just heard that her close friend has died – a friend whom she and Giovanni had visited in hospital in the opening scenes of the film. So this is Lidia's situation: she has just heard of the death of one of her close friends and then she witnesses her husband's flirtation with infidelity.

What is essential in this scene is that this situation is not one of Lidia's making – at the very least, that is what the film is trying to point to: these are not problems *caused by* the moral failures of humans; rather, they are *things that happen*, just as a new day will follow the night of this film, just as rain will fall (as happens later during the film's night), so too will infidelities occur and people close to us die. Antonioni is not trying to condemn Giovanni or Valentina or Lidia for their actions or lack of actions. Instead, he is charting occurrences, making us observe them without being called upon to judge these happenings. These are some of the reasons why Deleuze refers to Antonioni's films as ones that adopt an 'objective' point of view.

There is also the great sense here of Lidia being emptied out – she's reduced to *degree zero* might be one way of putting it. As Deleuze himself writes, in general of Antonioni's films,

> What happen[s] is that, from one result to the next, the characters [are] objectively emptied: they are suffering less from an absence of one another than from their absence from themselves . . . . Hence this space [the 'empty space' of Antonioni's films] refers back to the lost gaze of the being who is absent from the world as much as from himself (Deleuze, 1989, p. 9).

The lost gaze of the being who is absent from the world: such as Lidia's state at this point of *La Notte*, as much as it echoes Irene in *Europa '51*, the maid in *Umberto D* or even Antonio in *Bicycle Thieves*.

Again we need to ask why this is significant. These humans whom Deleuze describes as being absent from the world and absent from themselves; might this merely echo like the reiteration of a thousand other commentators on Antonioni, that he charts a modernist, existential alienation which features humans in various states of late capitalist angst? Certainly, yes, but Deleuze also wants to try to argue that Antonioni is a profoundly optimistic director who believes in the kinds of positivities opened up by modern existence. To reduce characters and humans to a degree zero is indeed a positive thing, a necessary thing, and it is one of the central claims of Deleuze's philosophy as a whole. While Antonioni offers a devastating critique of modern life, by way of this critique he also opens up the possibility of redeeming or rediscovering that modern world. We must absent ourselves from the world modernity has created in order to be reborn into a new one and to discover what might be possible in a different kind of world. It is as though Antonioni's films are saying something like – yes, we could go on being unhappy with ourselves, with our relationships, with our ways of life, or we could realize, as he urges his characters to do, just how awful and intolerable that world is. Only if we are awake to that horror will we then have the capacity to redress that horror and begin the process of building or discovering something else. 'Men's only hope', Deleuze asserts at one point, 'lies in a revolutionary becoming: the only way of casting off their shame or responding to what is intolerable' (Deleuze, 1995, p. 171). Thus, Deleuze will argue that 'Antonioni does not criticize the modern world, in whose possibilities he profoundly believes' (ibid., 1989, p. 204).

On this basis it is evident that the endings of Antonioni's films are reassuringly optimistic. The ending of *L'avventura*, for example, points to the possible reconciliation of the couple when the woman gently caresses the man's hair. In *Blow Up*, the closing scene is surely also a justifiably famous one. The film unfolds in roughly the following way: a photographer named Thomas (David Hemmings), while idly taking some photographs in a park one day, later discovers that he seems to have photographed a murder. Following a long process of blowing up and developing reams of photographs, he isolates what unequivocally seems to be the image of a murdered body lying beneath a tree. He even returns to the park and discovers the dead body lying precisely where the photograph designated it would be. However, upon returning home he finds all of the photographs have been stolen and thus all evidence of the crime has been erased. As a result, all of his intrigues and investigations have come to nothing: again Antonioni shows us a character who is left with the same kind of emptiness that encompassed Lidia in *La Notte*. At the end of the film, our hero is wandering home on foot and he comes across a group of rebellious agitators who have emerged once or twice before during the film (these characters seem to be broadly representative of protest movements of the 1960s). But here, in peace and quiet, they play a mime game of tennis, pretending to hit a tennis ball back and forth on a tennis court, but without a tennis ball. One of these characters hits the imaginary ball over the fence of the court and the ball lands imaginarily near where our hero is walking. The tennis mimes gesture to the hero to throw the non-existent ball back to them. Verily, he walks over to the ball and tosses it back to them. Moments later, we hear the sound of a tennis racket hitting a ball, the 'pink, ponk' of a tennis match, including the 'thuds' with which the ball bounces off the court: the imaginary tennis ball seems to have become real enough to produce sounds that we can all hear (and the subjective has become objective, the imaginary has become real).

There are a great number of interpretations of this scene (see Brunette's summation, 1998, pp. 124–6), but I think the reasonably straightforward way to interpret it is to declare, on the basis of the social construction of meaning – the fact that if a society agrees to call this a game of tennis, then for all intents and purposes it is a game of tennis – humans do have the ability to build the kind of world that might satisfy them. Humans do not need to accept the meanings of things that have been decreed to them or passed down by their elders, they are capable of inventing or reinventing meanings. If one finds the world intolerable, then one can also discover that meanings need not always miss their mark and communication need not be futile or always estranging. Rather, meaning and significance can be worthwhile and can result in the creation of a meaningful world, to the point of producing the sound of racket on ball, even when there are no such objects. Such is the point of the film: that even though our hero has gone through the emptiness, blankness and futility of the murder mystery, there is hope that there will be a future in which humans will discover a world worthy of being shared, that they will be able to create beliefs worth sharing and appreciating, even an appreciation of an imaginary game of tennis.

The ending of *L'eclisse* is equally famous, perhaps even more so: a seven minute montage sequence of objects and spaces of varying metaphorical significance. It is as though the entire film, which we might have thought was leading somewhere, to a realization of love in which each of the lovers would discover the other's worth and discover a new world together, suddenly ends in nothing, leads nowhere, runs out of steam and fails to deliver on its promise. Instead of filming the couple's planned meeting, which has failed to occur, the camera finds other objects: 'the coming of the evening, a bus, the headlines of a newspaper, a woman with a pram, a trotting horse being exercised, a drum with water slowly leaking from a hole, a lawn sprinkler pulsating, a building under construction, the sound of the wind and the sight of it shaking spring acacia blooms' (Rohdie, 1990, p. 115). Again, a Deleuzian approach to these scenes would see its consequences as positive: the world goes on and has a beauty and power beyond the frivolities and tribulations of the humans we have encountered. This world, we might imagine the film to be saying, deserves or needs to be discovered anew; we have lost our characters (our subjects), but because of this, we are able to rediscover the world (its objects). If the world as it currently is, the world as signified by the characters and situations we have come across in this film, needs to be dissolved and evacuated, then correlatively, as a consequence of this, it can be rediscovered and reborn; indeed, the world *needs* to be re-shaped away from the kinds of human concerns that have made it so unendurable and that the film's love affairs and human interests amplify so pointedly. The world needs to be eclipsed, as it were. As Deleuze himself claims of Antonioni's films, near the end of the book on the time-image, for Antonioni, 'The world awaits its inhabitants, who are still lost in neurosis' (Deleuze, 1989, p. 205). Needless to say, Deleuze's sentiments seem to be best expressed by Pascal Bonitzer's stunning summation:

There is no more beautiful moment in an Antonioni film (and each seems structured to this end) than that in which his characters, his human beings, are cancelled, only so as to leave behind, it seems, a space without attributes, a pure space [. . .]. Empty space is not a void: full of mists, of fleeting faces, of evanescent presences or of random movements, this space represents that final point of being finally freed from the negativity of intentions, of passions, of human existence (Bonitzer in Brunette 1998, p. 89).

6

The Time-Image (II): Ophüls and Fellini

The Time of the Time-Image

Why is the time-image called the time-image? In the previous chapter, we saw how character and plot function in films like *Bicycle Thieves* and Antonioni's *Blow Up*, *L'eclisse* and others. That is, we saw how characters come to be stopped in their tracks, alienated, confused and emptied out. We also saw how the plots of these films are somewhat open-ended, lacking in definitive closure or resolution. They also lack strong centralizing plots and instead seem to wander with no particular aim or goal in mind. But how do these attributes add up to something called a 'time-image'? Why would such films be placed in a category called the time-image instead of being another sub-category of the movement-image? In short, what does time have to do with the time-image?

In very general terms, Deleuze makes such films examples of the time-image because the characters in them are forced to ask questions on their past. Antonio does so in *Bicycle Thieves*, as he questions his place in the world and his relations with the other members of his family, and he is concerned furthermore about his future, his prospects. Characters in Antonioni's films do likewise: Lidia questions her relations with her husband, the photographer queries what has happened to him in *Blow Up*, the woman in *L'eclisse* worries about her life and her loves. And yet, might we claim that similar questions arise in *On the Waterfront*, a film that exemplifies the large form of the action-image? And might the same be said for *Stagecoach* (the Ringo Kid settles his score with the past) or *Sergeant Rutledge* (which is all about revisiting and restoring the past)? Important distinctions need to be made here. These latter films, films which are of the movement-image, return to the past or question the past in the hope of *closing down the past*: they search the past in order to find definitive answers in that past: Terry will discover his self-betrayal in his past; the Ringo Kid will finally put the past 'to rest' by killing the Plummer brothers; Rutledge will clear his name by uncovering a past without prejudice. By contrast, films of the time-image go into the past *in order to open up the past*, to render it malleable and questionable, and also to allow it to become retrievable and open to reinvention. Time-image films go into the past in order to enter that past as a zone of experimentation.

Initially, there are two ways in which Deleuze explains how the time-image takes effect. From C. S. Pierce a new type of perception is configured, which the time-image introduces, while from Bergson a new relation to the past is discovered, which emerges in the time-image. In *Cinema 1*, Deleuze develops his understanding of the types of images from Peirce's conceptions of firstness, secondness and thirdness: firstness is expressed by the affection-image, secondness by the perception-image and thirdness by the relation-image (we have seen how the latter functions in Hitchcock's films). But the time-image, Deleuze claims, calls for a new understanding of perception, an understanding of perception that is not directly related to action. Therefore, extending Peirce's categories of the image, Deleuze introduces a founding term: *zeroness*. Instead of a perception-image now being conceived merely in terms of movement – of perception and responses to that perception – Deleuze now proposes a perception-image, which perceives both a movement itself as well as the distance moved; that is, the 'interval' of movement. There are two steps to this conception:

(a) the perception of movement as it happens; and

(b) a perception of the movement as a whole; that is, in terms of the distance a movement traverses in time and space.

In other words, if I see a baseball thrown from the pitcher to the catcher, then I can perceive this ball as it moves (my perception of the 'experience' of the ball as it moves), but I will also perceive the movement as a whole – its movement from pitcher's mound to catcher's mitt – which Deleuze calls the interval of movement. The ball's movement 'in the present' is added to a notion of its movement as perceived in time and space; it is a combination of the (a) + (b) noted above. Deleuze proposes to call this a category of zeroness, as that which underpins all the other categories of the image.

The other categories of the image can be then reconceived in these terms: firstness, the affection-image, emerges in the interval which is traversed by a movement (in the 'what' that happens or in the 'will it happen?' while the ball moves from the pitcher to the catcher – we might ponder, for example, whether the batter will hit the ball). Secondness, the action-image, is conceived in causal terms; that is, of discerning *how* the movement occurs (what is the action that makes a movement happen? By virtue of what action does the ball get from the pitcher to the catcher, and how does it achieve this in such a way that the batter does not hit the ball?). In this way it is the action which 'performs' a movement. Thirdness, the relation-image, is an accounting for the movement as a whole: the movement itself, as well as the interval traversed during the course of the movement – the relation-image questions how it is that all the pieces fit together (see Deleuze, 1989, pp. 30–2).

Most important for the time-image is the reconception of perception: from here, the perception-image no longer belongs to the category of secondness (as it does for the movement-image). Instead, it functions in the category of zeroness, that is, as pure optical and sound situations, where a character sees and hears, but can no longer act or relate, while affection-images will no longer lead to definitive actions. Indeed, the entire semiotic of the time-image constructed by Deleuze is markedly different from that defined by the movement-image. Its beginning point is perception, but its end point is no longer action. Its end point is memory.

Time, Memory and the Past

If, for the movement-image, perception is related to action then for the time-image, perception is related to memory. For the movement-image, what one sees is always related to one's eventual response in an action. If I see an injustice being done then it is my duty to respond to that injustice with an action, to bring the perpetrators of the crime to justice, and to see that good triumphs over evil. Little of this happens for the time-image. Instead, what I see becomes linked with memory: I see something, and it takes me back to the past, it summons up the past: and there I stand, trying to discern the relations between past, present and future. It is in this way that a new kind of perception-image comes to stand at the foundation of the time-image: I perceive the thing as it is, but I also try to discern its passage through time and space.

Another way to conceive this distinction is by way of Bergson's differentiation between habitual memory and attentive memory (see Bergson, 1988, pp. 110–1). Habitual memories are the ones that I make no effort to recall, they come to me automatically, and they do so because I have refined these memories in such a way that they can emerge in me automatically. I have taken that path, for example, from my front door to the train station so many times that I no longer need to think about how it is that I get there. Instead, it comes to me automatically; it is so well-rehearsed and buried in my 'memory bank' that it comes to me without any effort. Bergson's example is that of understanding spoken words: when I hear someone say 'house', that auditory perception is immediately shaped by memory into a recognizable word: I automatically 'know', as it were, what I am hearing. This is habitual memory, and it is habitual memory which the movement-image tries to refine. But why might this be an example of the kind of logic which inspires the movement-image? Characters in the films of the movement-image desire to perform actions with the least resistance, that is, to perform actions well so that a solution to a problem will be enacted. The best way to ensure this will be the case is to ensure that the necessary actions will in some way be 'hard wired' – the gunfighter-hero is always the one with the quickest draw, the one whose skills have been honed to perfection so that his movements happen automatically, with the least amount of resistance (we have seen this with the Ringo Kid in *Stagecoach* and Jim Deakins in *The Big Sky*). The final goal of the movement-image is one in which all actions are pre-designed or pre-programmed – automatic – so that perception's links with action will be pure and untroubled; the future will happen automatically because of the refinements a character or hero has made to perception's links with action; the past will have been clarified and so is no longer open to question.

Attentive memory is very different from this. We see something but we do not know immediately what it is. Rather, we need to dig back into our memory in order to discern what it might be (see Mullarkey, 1999, pp. 49–50). Attentive memory is thus intrinsically related to time: here, to see something opens up time. By invoking such a form of memory, you might indeed discover what it is that you see, just as Proust's narrator discovered he was indeed seeing and tasting a madeleine (Proust, 1992, p. 60). But what that discovery opens up is far more important than simply identifying the object invoked. It is, for the time-image, as much as it was for Proust, the discovery of a new kind of world, a new way of seeing and perceiving things.

Max Ophüls: *Letter from an Unknown Woman, Lola Montès, La ronde*

One way to conceive of this distinction is to declare that while characters in films of the movement-image aim to perform actions, characters in films of the time-image aim to perform memories. Nowhere might this be more evident than in the films of Max Ophüls, especially his two great memory circuit films, *La ronde* (1950) and *Lola Montès* (1955). What is perhaps Ophüls's most famous film, *Letter from an Unknown Woman* (1948), presents us, however, with a slightly different case, and it is from here that our analysis can begin.

In *Letter from an Unknown Woman*, the heroine Lisa writes a letter to the man she has loved from afar for many years, the concert pianist Stefan Brand. Set in Vienna in the early years of the twentieth century, the film unfolds according to a series of flashbacks cued by the letter, chronicling the relationship between Lisa and Stefan over a decade or more, including such events, for example, as a passionate night spent together, the result of which was a child for Lisa, a consequence that Stefan had been entirely unaware of before reading Lisa's letter. Might this not be a time-image then, for does this film not push back into a past that is discovered anew? It is true that we have a newly discovered past – Stefan is confronted with a past of which he had been almost entirely unaware, so that the past is rediscovered anew for him. However, in *Letter from an Unknown Woman*, the past is discovered only in so far as that past can be *put in its place*: Stefan discovers how he has wasted his life, that he could have found happiness with this woman who was utterly devoted to him, that if he had not been so selfish and unknowing, the mistakes of his past would not have been committed – for now his career as a pianist has come to naught and for a final indiscretion he is faced with the prospect of a duel in which he will almost certainly be killed. Indeed, the letter fixes his purpose: he decides to turn up to the duel and face the consequences: his past has been put in its place, and now he feels he must 'face the music'; the mistakes and ignorance of his past can only have one justifiable outcome, for death is the only consequence his behaviour deserves. It is in this way that *Letter from an Unknown Woman* securely places the past, present and future into a solid, unchanging relation. Rather than providing a time-image, this film is an exemplary movement-image.

In *Lola Montès*, by contrast, the story is told from the perspective of the present by way of an exploration of the past – that of the life and times of Lola Montès. But there is little sense that the past created there is in any way a true or definitive past; rather, it is a past of legend, insinuation and adventure. And even if any events depicted there are accurate, they are nevertheless recreated as part of a show – they are not recollection-flashbacks in the manner of *Letter from an Unknown Woman*. All the events take place as part of a circus show or variety entertainment, the subject of which is the life of Lola Montès. But the aging Lola is herself the central star of this entertainment-recreation of her own life. As a result, each episode from the past is also a replay of that past in the present, so that Lola in the past is simultaneously played by Lola in the present. And thus we see the layers of time built up before us as a kind of kaleidoscope of dazzling, intertwining facets of Lola's life. These layers are held together by the unfolding diagnosis throughout the film of Lola's faltering heart condition, as though these layers of her past were so many layers of her heart's experiences. At the end of the film, we do discover that, indeed, Lola has been suffering from a broken heart, for Lola's true love with the King of Bavaria (a married noble) was never allowed to flourish.

La ronde, in a similar way, revisits a past – turn of the century Vienna (like *Letter from an Unknown Woman* in this) to relate a series of interlinked romantic episodes. The film opens with a song of the carousel being sung by the man who operates the carousel. The carousel is itself a stand-in for the cinema machine, turning round and round, and its operator is a stand-in for the filmmaker, for it is he who orchestrates and assists the romantic adventures that unfold throughout the film. The film's first episode – 'The tart and the soldier' – shows us a soldier out from his barracks one night who is opportunely targeted by a prostitute. When they are just about to get down to business, our carousel operator, in the guise of a soldier, blows the bugle to summon all soldiers back to the barracks, thus stopping short the romantic interlude. Following the first episode, the soldier embarks on his next conquest, that of the young maid Mademoiselle Marie, and once this romance reaches its conclusion, our narrator–operator–filmmaker then takes Marie by the hand and declares to her, 'we're going on a stroll through time'. There (two months forward in time), another romantic encounter awaits Marie and what the film calls 'the rich young man', Alfred. Again, our filmmaker–carousel operator assists in the mechanisms of love, and the film follows a number of episodes in this fashion: Alfred next falls for a married woman, then we follow the married woman's relationship with her husband, then the husband and what our narrator–operator calls the 'sweet young thing', and so on. Finally, at the end of the film, an actress has an affair with a count, the latter being a high-ranking soldier of some sort. This couple chats frankly about sensual pleasures as they fall to bed, only for the film to deliver a hushed 'ahem!' as we cut to the narrator–carousel operator editing strips of film, thus kindly censoring the sexual act for us: the carousel operator's role as proxy filmmaker is here made explicit. The count, on his way back to his barracks after his romantic encounter, then passes Franz, the original romantic soldier of the film, and thus, as our narrator tells us, 'the circuit is closed. It's story', he adds, 'is ours'.

Each of these films exhibits the expansion of memory and the past from an opening perception – a fluttering heart (*Lola Montès*), a carousel (*La ronde*) – to expose layers and levels and facets of the past, each one acting upon the others so as to form . . . to form what? They form what Deleuze refers to as a crystal-image.

The Crystal-Image

Where does the present end and the past begin? This is the question central to Deleuze's notion of the crystal-image. And his answer, adapted from Bergson is quite simply that it is very difficult to tell where the line between the present and the past can be drawn. To declare that something is 'now' is to already have opened up this now to its own passing. As the baseball enters the catcher's mitt, I have already wedded that particular moment to the ones that have preceded it: the baseball's being thrown by the pitcher, its passing the bat and, finally, this moment of being gloved by the catcher. This one moment in the present also stretches into the past, just as Lola's troubled heart opens onto a past of myriad encounters of the heart, and the carousel keeps on turning, drawing more and more folds into its circuit. And what, at any rate, is a baseball, or a heart or a carousel? We know these objects and we can see them in the present. But we only know them because we have also known them in the past: the baseball we see in the present is thus also composed of so many baseballs we have seen in the past. What we see and experience in the present invariably involves going into the past at the same time (and this is true whether we invoke either habitual or attentive memory).

Ronald Bogue provides a fine example of this splitting of past and present (Bogue, 2003, p. 139). What happens, he asks, when I have lost a key? The moment in the present is that of *my key is lost*. But this must also be combined with the notion that, in the past, I had this key and I know that there are certain things I have done with this key in the past. Perhaps, Bogue continues, if I can work out what I did with it in the past I will be better able to work out where it is in the present. And finally, along with this lost key in the present and the key I had in the past, I will have a vision or sense of having the key again – of finding it – at some point in the future. Time thus has the capacity to split in all of these ways: from a present back into a past that was and into a future to come. This example also clearly shows us the distinction between habitual and attentive memory. *Not* losing the key would most likely lead us into habitual memory: I would use my key to open the lock and I would do so habitually, without really 'thinking' about it. But to lose the key opens up to something else: I have to search, go back into my past, wander about in its episodes, in order that I might discover where that key might be. This putting oneself back into the past is precisely what occurs by way of attentive memory.

Bergson has his own example of the splitting of past and present of which Deleuze makes use – that of an actor trying to remember his lines and play a part:

> [T]here is a recollection of the present, contemporaneous with the present itself, as closely coupled as a role to an actor. [Quoting from Bergson]: 'Our actual existence, then, whilst it is unrolled in time, duplicates itself along with a virtual existence, a mirror image. Every moment of our life presents these two aspects, it is actual and virtual, the object on one side and its reflexion on the other . . . Whoever becomes conscious of the continual duplicating into perception and memory . . . will compare himself to an actor playing his part automatically, listening to himself and beholding himself play' (Deleuze, 1989, p. 79; translation modified).[1]

Deleuze takes Bergson's insight here in a direction that emphasizes its conception of time: the actor's playing his part *in the present* while also listening to or observing himself *as though looking at himself 'in the past'* delivers 'a little time in the pure state'. Such is the kind of experience which Deleuze takes as exemplary of the time-image: time splits into past and present, not in order that one might then be able to declare that this is where the present ends and the past begins, but rather so that one can declare that past and present are always dividing, always splitting, so that each carries the other along with it. For Deleuze, this is what is called 'the crystal-image':

> What constitutes the crystal-image is the most fundamental operation of time: since the past is not constituted after the present that it was but at the same time, time has to split itself in two at each moment as present and past [. . .] Time consists of this split, and it is this, time, that we *see in the crystal* (Deleuze, 1989, p. 81).

Ophüls' films exemplify the crystal-image, the construction of interlinked strands between Lola's present and past in *Lola Montès*, between the distinct episodes and the narrator's orchestration of those episodes in *La ronde*. Both of these films begin from points of splitting (the 'splitting' of Lola's heart; the turning of the carousel) and construct grand crystalline formations, what Deleuze will declare are examples of 'the perfect, completed crystal' (Deleuze, 1989, p. 83). In these films, no one can be quite sure where the present ends and the past begins. *Letter from an Unknown Woman*, by contrast, finds its end point: the splitting of past and present in that film is an occasion for ensuring that past and present remain separate and distinct. Knowing what the past has been, Stefan now knows what he must do in the present and the future.

Federico Fellini

If Ophüls constructs perfect crystals, then Fellini's films typically begin with a simple crystal only to expand, layer by layer, the complexity of the crystalline structure. For Deleuze, Fellini's films present 'the crystal caught in its state of growth' (Deleuze, 1989, p. 88). And surely alongside Resnais (with whom we deal in the following chapter), Fellini is the great auteur of memory, of the splitting of time into present and past. In *8½* (1963), Guido's (Marcello Mastroianni) existence in the present is overlaid with memories of his past which in turn assert themselves as visions in the present. And this character is also a filmmaker so that visions of his past are re-imagined for the film he is trying to make. By way of these interlinked representational layers – memory, fantasy, dream, film, photograph, screen test and sketch – Fellini slowly builds his crystal-image. Entwined with these representational layers, however, are also the layers of Guido's past: his memories of his parents, of La Saraghina (the first siren who awakened the young Guido's sexual appetites), the Church which offers him constant moral points of reference, not to mention the myriad past loves who swamp his memories and who are so evocatively rendered in the fantastical, magisterial harem-fantasy sequence, whereby all his past loves faithfully serve and worship Guido (the fantasy of a world constructed solely for him).

The film's conclusion and Guido's reconciliation with his wife Luisa do not signal that Guido has now renounced his past and put it behind him, that all is forgiven as he confesses the errors of his ways. No such thing occurs. Instead, Guido accepts his fate: if his memories and visions have constructed a grand crystal (as indeed they have from a Deleuzian perspective), then this crystalline construction is to be embraced, praised and celebrated – it is not something to be ashamed of, in other words. The glittering circus-carnival atmosphere of the film's closing minutes, beneath the enormous stage set that has been constructed for the spaceship of the film within a film, offers us a crystal-image of glittering richness. Within this, Guido turns to Luisa to ask for forgiveness and he admits to her, 'I've been a fraud'. But he adds, '[t]his confusion is me . . . '. He is happy that the past remains open, that he can face the future, even as he knows the crystal will keep growing, that past and present will continue to split . . . 'This confusion is me'.

Giulietta degli spiriti (1965) treads a similar path. The married, middle-aged Giulietta (Giulietta Masina), suspecting her husband of infidelity, slowly builds for herself a model of her life as it has been and as it could be. As one commentator has noted, '[i]n *Giulietta degli spiriti*, as in *8½*, Fellini employs a series of stunningly beautiful sequences that represent fantasies, daydreams, visions and flashbacks to show the viewer how Giulietta's past impinges upon her present' (Bondanella, 1992, p. 302). These levels unfold by way of multiple intertwining episodes and characters: the repeated memory of a school play where Giulietta played a Christian martyr burned by Romans; her memories of her grandfather's elopement with a circus performer (the 'woman on the trapeze'); the séance near the beginning of the film where we are first made aware of Giulietta's kinship with the 'spirits'; her friendship with her erotically adventurous neighbour, Susy; her relationship to her mother and sisters; her visit to the Eastern mystic; her enlistment of a private detective to spy on, film and photograph her husband; her attempted confrontation with her husband's lover. Like Guido in *8½*, by the time we reach the end of the film, Giulietta's relationship to the crystal the film has constructed is one of acceptance, of discovery and rebirth and kinship with the crystal that now envelops her. Fellini has put it eloquently enough himself:

> Giulietta alone, at the end of the film, should mean the discovery of an individuality. The thing she feared the most, the departure of her husband, is revealed as a gift of providence. Giulietta will no longer depend on the paternal figure of [her husband], who has, nonetheless, enriched her life. To him, too, as everyone and everything, Giulietta feels grateful because they all – even those who seem the most fearful enemies – helped the process of her liberation. (Quoted in Bondanella, 1992, p. 306).[2]

Again, the construction of the crystal entails an acceptance of its layers and complexities.

Roma (1972) presents the city of Rome as a crystal, of multiple facets, entrances and exits. 'The only unity of Rome', writes Deleuze, 'is that of the spectacle which connects all its entrances. The spectacle becomes universal', he continues, 'and keeps on growing, precisely because it has no object other than entrances into the spectacle' (Deleuze, 1989, p. 89). The film jumps from one historical period to another, from the spectacle of eating at a restaurant during the fascist period, to the building of an underground subway system in the 1970s, which in turn leads to the unearthing of Ancient Roman frescoes (the past in the present) whose images magically and tragically fade right before the camera's eyes, as though literalizing for us the splitting of past and present: the past, newly discovered as a product of the present, splits and becomes the past once more, a mere memory of the present.

The crystal in Fellini's films, Deleuze argues, 'is always in the process of formation, expansion, which makes everything it touches crystallize, and to which its seeds give a capacity for indefinite growth' (Deleuze, 1989, p. 89). If Ophüls' films deliver 'perfect crystals', while Fellini's catch crystals in the process of their formation, then Deleuze also refers to two other types of the crystal-image. In the films of Jean Renoir, the crystal is displayed, but it is displayed only in so far as it will be revealed to be flawed: in Renoir's films there is a crack in the crystal, and it is by way of the crack that an escape from the crystal can be found. In contrast, therefore, to the magnificent crystals of Ophüls or Fellini, where the aim is to lodge oneself within the crystal, to celebrate and enjoy the crystal, for Renoir the aim is to get out of the crystal, to find its fault or crack, by means of which an escape can be made, like the poacher at the beginning of *La Marseillaise* (1938) who jumps through the courtroom window and escapes into the French Revolution (see Rushton, 2011b). The fourth and final type of crystal is the crystal in the process of decay or decomposition: the films of Luchino Visconti. *The Leopard* (1963), for example, presents a most dramatic and luscious crystal, whose dazzling accomplishments and prizes are slowly becoming worthless, out of time and out of their time, as though the crystalline forms of the present are slowly crumbling into the past, right before our eyes.

7

The Time-Image (III): Welles and Resnais

The Actual and the Virtual

What does Deleuze mean by the *actual* and the *virtual*? These are terms I have been reluctant to mention until now, because they are terms fraught with misinterpretation. The first trap is this: to conceive of the actual as that which is real, while the virtual is what is unreal, fake, imagined, illusory or pretend. To conceive of the actual–virtual split in this way is to misunderstand Deleuze. The second trap is to proclaim that the movement-image privileges the actual while the time-image privileges the virtual. This too is an incorrect assumption. The third mistake is to think Deleuze's aim is to downplay the actual so that he can instead praise and advocate the virtual. This again is a mistake. Instead, what Deleuze explains in the *Cinema* books are the different kinds of relation between the actual and the virtual, for there is no actual without a virtual alongside it, while correlatively, where we find the virtual we will also find the actual. It is the relation between the actual and the virtual that is key for Deleuze.

Let us begin with a proposition, then: *the actual is present, the virtual is past*. In other words, if the actual is what is happening to me in the present, then the virtual is composed of my memories of things that have happened to me in the past. Following Bergson, Deleuze claims that, for much of the time, our memories are attempts 'to actualize the virtual' (Deleuze, 1989, p. 54); that is, we try to remember something in order to drag it away from being a 'mere' memory so as to make it something more concrete instead. In Ford's *Sergeant Rutledge* (discussed in Chapter 3), the aim of the trial is for Rutledge to try to drag his memories from being merely *his* memories into the realm of public scrutiny and public truth; that is, to make his innocence actual, true. The use of flashback in films of the movement-image is usually a strategy of transforming the virtual into the actual. But not all virtuals will become actualized: in *Sergeant Rutledge*, it might have been possible that it was indeed Rutledge who committed rape and murder, and the prosecuting attorney certainly acts to prove that this is the case: he wants to try to prove that the virtual past in which Rutledge is a rapist and murderer can be proven to be true, so that it is *this* virtual which becomes actualized. And yet, as we know, the film does not turn out like that, and the virtual past in which Rutledge is guilty *remains virtual*: it is never actualized, while what is actualized is his innocence. Thus, if the film begins with two virtuals – one in which Rutledge is guilty and another in which he is innocent – then the task of the film to discover which of these virtuals can be actualized, on the one hand, and which will remain virtual, on the other. Ultimately, this forging of clear distinctions between the actual and the virtual is central to the movement-image: there are virtuals which will be declared false ('Rutledge is guilty') while there are virtuals which will be discovered to be true ('Rutledge is innocent'). To find out what is true and actual and what is false and virtual is one of the chief aims of films of the movement-image. This, then, is the kind of relation between the actual and the virtual which the movement-image affirms: *the actual is true while the virtual is false*. (We shall wait to see what the time-image does with these terms.)

A second claim: *the virtual is subjective, the actual is objective*. As D. N. Rodowick describes, 'the actual refers to the states of things – the physical and the real – as described in space through perception. The virtual', continues Rodowick, 'is subjective, that is, mental and imaginary, sought out in time through memory' (Rodowick, 1997, p. 92). The actual therefore refers to things that many subjects might be able to agree on as being a 'state of things', just as a courtroom and a society agree that Rutledge is innocent at the conclusion of *Sergeant Rutledge*. The virtual, by contrast, are those things an individual subject might be able to propose or imagine, but which cannot claim an 'objective' existence. Deleuze will even go so far as to declare outright that 'the actual is always objective, but the virtual is subjective' (Deleuze, 1989, p. 83). And yet, we should not be too hasty to jump to simple conclusions here. Let us read very closely with Deleuze:

> . . . the confusion of the real and the imaginary is a simple error of fact, and does not affect their discernibility: the confusion is produced solely 'in someone's head'. But indiscernibility constitutes an objective illusion; it does not suppress the distinction between the two sides, but makes it unattributable, each side taking the other's role in a relation which we must describe as a reciprocal presupposition [. . .]. In fact, there is no virtual which does not become actual in relation to the actual, the latter becoming virtual through the same relation [. . .]. The indiscernibility of the real and the imaginary, or of the present and the past, of the actual and the virtual, is definitely not produced in the head or the mind, it is the objective characteristic of certain existing images which are by nature double (ibid., p. 69).

Deleuze's claims here are somewhat rushed and inexact, as though he is trying to explain too many things all at once. First of all he is describing what occurs for the movement-image: when the confusion between the real and the imaginary is 'in someone's head', we can be sure we are on the terrain of the movement-image. Secondly, he then goes on to describe what occurs for the time-image, that is, when the distinction between the real and the imaginary becomes indiscernible in an objective way. Here, in the time-image, there is no longer merely confusion between the real and the imaginary 'in someone's head'; instead, the indiscernibility between the real and the imaginary, the present and the past, the actual and the virtual, becomes an objective 'fact'. As Deleuze states, when this occurs, what was virtual now becomes actual while what was actual correlatively becomes virtual: the actual and virtual become entwined to the point where we can no longer tell which is which.

Let us determine how these entwinements of the actual and the virtual function in the movement-image on the one hand and the time-image on the other. As we have seen, in *On the Waterfront*, Terry Malloy is torn on the one hand between his allegiances to Johnny Friendly's mob, to his brother Charley and to the other workers on the waterfront who are 'protected' by Friendly and his gang, all of which constitute one bloc of allegiances. On the other hand he begins to develop along another path via his love for Edie, his interest in the teachings of the priest, and most of all, he realizes some of the choices he has made throughout his life might have been mistaken, he begins to understand that 'he could've been a contender' and that the practices of Friendly and his supporters might well have led him to lead a life of compromises, a life in which he was merely lying to himself; in short, he begins to suspect that he is living a lie. There is, if we follow Deleuze, a confusion 'inside Terry's head' between the real and the imaginary: in the past he had a chance of either winning the boxing match at Madison Square Garden and having a shot at the title, or of taking a dive and thus satisfying the betting scams of Johnny Friendly. Did he make the right choice? Did he make a *real* choice; or did he make a choice that, in retrospect, is now only an *imaginary* choice, a false choice, one which can now be judged as wrong, as the path he should not have chosen? Was his choice thus a choice of the virtual over the actual, so that ever since he has been living a virtual life, the life of a lie, a false existence – in short, he now discovers that he's 'been rattin' on himself all them years'. This is what the movement-image achieves: Terry realizes he has been living a virtual life, and he comes to a realization in which this confusion between virtual and actual was merely a confusion inside his head – he believed he had actually been living his own life, but how he understands that what he thought was actual really was virtual, that he had been confused 'inside his head' about what was actual and what was virtual. Near the end of the film, after his brother has been murdered, the objective reality of the distinction between the actual and the virtual is made clear: Terry has been living a lie, he has been enveloped by the falseness of the virtual, and now he will testify against Johnny Friendly and thus prove to himself, to the other characters and to those who view the film, that the distinction between the actual and the virtual is clear and objective; that Terry should have been a contender, that Johnny Friendly and his cronies are crooks who have been holding back not only Terry's life and happiness, but the happiness and lives of the other workers on the waterfront. The film's triumphant ending is a triumph of the actual over the virtual, a declaration that the virtual lies of the past can be clearly separated from the actual truths of the present: 'let's go to work!'. (And the actuality of the American dream is reaffirmed).

In contrast to *On the Waterfront*, Orson Welles's extraordinary film, *Citizen Kane* (1941), one of the founding landmarks of the time-image for Deleuze, posits a very different relation between the actual and the virtual. Its guiding question is: what is the truth of 'Rosebud', and by extension, what is the truth of Charles Foster Kane? In his attempts to answer these questions, the investigator named Thompson digs up the many layers of Kane's past, a number of 'virtuals', some of which might be true, others which might be false. Or, to put it another way, the truth of any of the claims is not at stake, so it is not a question of the true versus the false. At the end of the film, none of the characters gets to know what 'Rosebud' was, and yet viewers of the film do: the camera shows us the sledge named Rosebud as it burns in the fire, to disappear from the history so earnestly sought by the film's characters. Deleuze is, in fact, very precise in his discussions of *Citizen Kane*:

> The scheme of *Citizen Kane* may appear simple: Kane being dead, witnesses who offer their recollection-images in a series of subjective flashbacks are questioned. But it is more complex than this. The investigation is focused on 'Rosebud' (what is it? of what does this word mean?). And the investigator who carries out soundings; each of the witnesses questioned will be equivalent to slice of Kane's life, a circle or sheet of virtual past, a continuum. And each time the question is: is it in this continuum, is it in this sheet, that lies the thing (the being) called Rosebud? [. . .] Rosebud will not be found in any of the regions explored, even though it is in one of them, in that of childhood, but so deeply buried that it is overlooked. Moreover, when Rosebud becomes embodied from its own movement in an image it is strictly *for nobody*, in the hearth where the discarded sledge burns (Deleuze 1989, p. 105, 111).

In contrast to the truths learnt in *On the Waterfront*, lessons which are intended for everybody – for the workers, for the priest, even for Friendly and his mob – the truth revealed at the end of *Citizen Kane* is *for nobody*, as Deleuze insists. And even if we, the viewers of the film, get to see what 'Rosebud' means, there is no way that this will be revealed as the truth of Kane's life. Might it be suggested that the theme, the 'truth' of the film, is that Kane lost his childhood, and that his ruthless ambitions were so many ways of trying to compensate for that loss? Such would be, perhaps, a psychoanalytic approach to the film's revelation (see Klein, 1998). But surely such an approach is too reductive (such is Deleuze's warning against seeing *Citizen Kane* as too simple). Rather, *Citizen Kane* is about all the layers that make up what we can know of Charles Kane, of 'what a man adds up to', so that no singular key word or object will be definitive; even 'Rosebud' reveals just another layer, a layer which might be true or false, just as all the other layers are.

Here, in *Citizen Kane*, the virtual is no longer merely subjective and the actual objective – the only actuality the film discerns is that Kane is dead. From this actual point in the present there then unfold layers of virtual past, and none of these layers of virtuality is ever definitively actualized. Certainly, some of the virtual images of Kane might be true, while others are surely false, but we can never know such distinctions as objective facts. Rather, the objective characteristic of the images of Kane is that the true and the false, the actual and the virtual cannot be discerned. Here, instead, as Deleuze writes, '[t]he indiscernibility of the real and the imaginary, or of the present and the past, of the actual and the virtual, is definitely not produced in the head or the mind, it is the objective characteristic of certain existing images which are by nature double' (Deleuze, 1989, p. 69).

Dreaming of an American Uncle

Why would anyone want to do such things? Why would anyone want to make a film in such a way? Can it not be said that life, enjoyment, truth and the good are much more easily accommodated by films like *On the Waterfront* or *Sergeant Rutledge*, for these are films which teach us lessons, they teach us how to separate right from wrong, the true from the false, and thus they show us how to lead a good life? Does it not therefore follow that a film like *Citizen Kane* is one that has given up on a vision of the good life and that it therefore has nothing to teach us? Does *Citizen Kane* merely demonstrate a nihilistic viewpoint, that there is no good life, and even if there were such a thing, we would not be able to discern what it was anyway? Is it this kind of nihilistic philosophy that is central to Deleuze's conception of the time-image, to refrain from action, to avoid affirming the good and the true? The answer to these questions is both yes and no. The time-image may no longer affirm the good or the true, but for Deleuze the time-image nevertheless is very much affirmative. We have discovered as much in our discussion of Antonioni's films as well as those of Fellini. Where, then, can the positivity of the time-image be located?

Alain Resnais's *Mon oncle d'Amérique* (1980) provides an excellent way of discerning the positivity of the time-image. The film is constructed around the interlinked biographies of three protagonists, Jean, Janine and René, while a fourth perspective is offered by a behavioural scientist, Henri Laborit. The latter is indeed a 'really existing' scientist about whom Resnais had originally desired to make a documentary. Laborit thus speaks from the perspective of the actual present, while the other three characters – characters that are fictional – illustrate various aspects of those theories by way of various episodes from their pasts. Here, then, is a first indicator of the 'sheets of past' exhibited by this film: we see our characters pass through the ages of youth, adolescence, into early adulthood and beyond. Class distinctions are also evident here: Jean (Roger Pierre), born in 1929, is from a relatively privileged background, is educated at the Sorbonne, inherits a large family estate and has little trouble relying on friends to reward him with key employment positions, most notably a government sponsored position he wins with the National Radio station. Janine (Nicole Garcia), on the other hand, born in 1948, is the daughter of communist leaning, working-class parents. Her early adult dream is to find success on the stage. Finally, René (Gérard Depardieu), born in 1941, is one of the sons in a family of peasant farmers whose ties with the land go back several generations. René breaks with his family in order to claw his way up the middle management ladder in a small Parisian textile firm.

There are already several layers of past in these interwoven lives. Resnais, however, adds further touches: the commentaries of Laborit, especially those where he explicitly invokes experiments conducted with rats, are illustrated by way of a number of rat scenarios, where the filmed behaviour of rats is intercut with the behavioural patterns of the three protagonists. Furthermore, each protagonist is guided or inspired by a film actor – Jean's is Danielle Darrieux; Janine's is Jean Marais, while René's idol is Jean Gabin – so that the film is additionally intercut with scenes and moments from the films of these actors in ways that mirror that actions and responses of the protagonists (see Wilson, 2006, p. 150).

As *Mon oncle d'Amérique* progresses through its ages, Jean is fired from his position in National Radio for political reasons, he leaves his wife (a lover since his youth) and has an extended affair with Janine (he moves in with her). Janine's life falls into a kind of limbo while she is enamoured of Jean, whereas René suffers his own difficulties in view of a company restructuring: he is relocated to Cholet in western France, 300 kilometres from his wife and children who choose to remain in Paris. Both Jean and René begin to suffer from health problems: Jean has a kidney disorder, while René suffers from stomach ulcers. And all the while we are receiving lessons in behavioural psychology from Laborit: the health difficulties being suffered by Jean and René are results, Laborit claims, of their inhibitions and defeats; the 'friend' who had originally won the National Radio position for Jean has now double-crossed him and gotten him fired, while René too had been defeated by a colleague in the competition for employment in his restructured workplace. These are outcomes, Laborit tells us, of the human being's 'natural' struggles for survival and equilibrium. To add grist to the mill, Jean's wife now confronts Janine, with whom she knows her husband is having an affair. Feigning a fatal illness, she tricks Janine into temporarily breaking off her affair with Jean. Jean then returns to the family home: his affair with Janine comes to an end.

A new sheet of past opens two years later. Janine happens upon Jean and discovers that his wife is alive and well. Janine is devastated: she has been deceived and she has lost the battle for Jean's love. At the same time, Janine is now working at the same firm as René. In collusion with another colleague, she effectively engineers René's dismissal. Faced with such a prospect, René tries to commit suicide.

Janine's confrontation with Jean is then set, but he declares that he is now happy living with his wife and that he could never have finished his book without having returned to his family – a commercially successful account of his period working at National Radio – and that, when all is said and done, he no longer needs Janine. Janine is devastated and angry. René, at the same time, has been revived and is recuperating in hospital. His wife visits and kisses him generously and evocatively – genuine signs of affection and compassion – scenes which are contrasted with intercut shots of Jean and Janine angrily fighting with and hitting each other (scenes which are further intercut with a staggering wild boar Jean has shot while hunting, scenes surely intended as references to Renoir's *La Règle du jeu* [1939]).

Laborit delivers his summation: that social conditioning, what our society rewards and punishes, is built up within us over our lifetimes. As we grow older, these behavioural tendencies grow ever stronger and 'more rigid, less and less subject to question'. Jean demonstrates the consequences of such rigid social conditioning: because of his social role and privileged upbringing, he can overcome adversity effectively by resisting change, by digging in his heels, by doing what is deemed proper (that is, returning to his wife, to the family home and by ensuring the nature of his inheritance). In this way he renounces his affair with Janine – a love which we are supposed to interpret as being in some way true or genuine – to instead take comfort in a more acceptable mode of existence (he returns to his wife), a mode of existence where no feathers are ruffled and social hierarchies are reinforced. Except, of course, that feathers are ruffled for Janine: she has no recourse to family history and social hierarchy, for she has long since broken with her proletarian family and had even curtailed her stage ambitions in order to pursue her love for Jean. From such a perspective she has clearly lost out. But she still possesses abilities for transformation: she successfully reinvents herself as a designer for the firm where René works, so that she stands as a character who can reinvent herself, experiment with roles, seek new horizons. And yet, as Loborit explains, our society, with its hierarchies and rigidities, punishes such people. Little wonder here that privilege wins out over the working classes.

René too strikes us as a figure of defeat. It is true that he makes an enormous break with his past by leaving the family farm, but nevertheless he also has difficulty changing with the times. Just as his father's farm had stubbornly stuck to the 'old ways', so too is René's management style old fashioned to the point where he is overlooked for promotion. And yet, even amidst his many defeats, a sympathetic portrait is painted of René. He is the only one of the three protagonists who refuses to double-cross an enemy; rather than stoop to the animal instinct of combativity – as Laborit demonstrates by way of his experiments with rats; the other two characters are left fighting at the film's end – René is the one character who seems genuinely to be loved by others at the film's conclusion (that is, by his wife and children). His suicide attempt is ultimately a strategy of transformation: René has had enough and now is the time for something entirely new. In the end, René is the character who possesses the possibility for total transformation.

What does all of this have to do with the time-image? *Mon oncle d'Amérique* is, Deleuze will claim, an exploration of various 'sheets of past'. The film charts the sheets through which the characters pass in order to show us the relations between those sheets and the transformations between sheets. As Deleuze argues, 'we make use of transformations which take place between two sheets to constitute a sheet *of* transformation' (Deleuze, 1989, p. 123). Therefore, *Mon oncle d'Amérique* is all about the relations between the sheets of past of each of the characters, the transformations which occur from one sheet to another, but also between the points in the present by means of which the sheets of past relate, that is, to Laborit's claims and the images of his rat experiments. Last but not least, there is the relation to the aspirational images of film stars that flows through each of the characters. Even, to make one last level or sheet, each of the characters' impressions or reminiscences of their American uncle (was he prosperous, or a failure, why did he go to America and so on?) opens up another layer of transformation. The charting of how these transformations occur, that is, the demonstration of how Janine moves from the theatre, to an affair with Jean, then to the textile factory, of how René moves from the farm, to the factory, then to Cholet, then to hospital and so on – is how the film shows us time itself: the relations between these sheets is a 'direct image of time'. Let us read with Deleuze:

> For instance, in a dream, there is no longer one recollection-image which embodies one particular point of a given sheet; there are a number of images which are embodied within each other, each referring to a different point of the sheet. Perhaps, when we read a book, watch a show, or look at a painting, and especially when we ourselves are the author, an analogous process can be triggered: we constitute a sheet of transformation which invests a kind of transverse continuity or communication between several sheets, and weaves a network of non-localizable relations between them. In this way we extract non-chronological time (Deleuze, 1989, p. 123).

In short, the relations and transformations between each of the sheets of past in *Mon oncle d'Amérique* constitute 'non-chronological time', 'a little time in the pure state'. These sheets can also be found in Resnais' other films, such as *Hiroshima, mon amour* (1959) (the relations between Hiroshima and Nevers) and *Muriel, or the Time of Return* (1963), but these layers of relations are also prominent in Welles: the series of interwoven and overlapping stories in *Mr Arkadin* (1955), *Touch of Evil* (1958) or *The Lady from Shanghai* (1947) all the way up to the masterful layers of *F for Fake* (1973).

Actual and Virtual, Past and Present: *Last Year in Marienbad* (1961)

Where now is the distinction between the actual and the virtual? In a film of the time-image, as *Mon oncle d'Amérique* is, the actual is put constantly into contact with the virtual: the sheets of past (virtual) are repeatedly brought together with Laborit's declamations of the present (actual), while images of an actual past are also put into contact with virtual pasts (that of the film star images) and virtual presents (the depictions of the rat experiments). These combinations – sheets, layers – reach their apogee when we see certain scenes from the film's past (such as when Jean walks out on his wife) repeated by the rats. *There is no longer any clear distinction between actual and virtual, past and the present.* Such is the relation between the actual and the virtual that the time-image affirms.

Nowhere is this relation between the actual and virtual portrayed more exceptionally than in Resnais's *Last Year in Marienbad*. Deleuze himself spends a great deal of time discussing this film, as do Rodowick and Bogue in their commentaries on the *Cinema* books (see Rodowick, 1997, pp. 100–108; Bogue, 2003, pp. 139–141; Deleuze 1989, pp. 116–124). From one perspective, *Last Year in Marienbad* is about 'peaks of present'; that is, everything takes place in the present, but the effort of the film is to reach back into the past so as to highlight the presentness, or potential presentness of the key events that are discovered in the past. Like Proust's madeleine from the past that magically reawakens him in the present, a past that comes to his narrator with the full force, touch and taste of the present (Proust, 1992, p. 60), then so too in *Last Year in Marienbad* does X (the man) try to deliver to A (the woman) the full force of their meeting last year in Marienbad, so that it might become present for her once again. X will therefore describe one event after another – 'in a garden at Friedrichsbad . . . near the statues . . . we looked at the fountain . . . you broke the heel of your shoe . . . I loved to hear you laugh . . . I went up to your room . . . it was so cold the fountains froze . . . ' – in the hope that, for A, these will form peaks of present, as though each were a glowing or burning memory that is buried but which might be revivified, brought back to presence. From the other perspective, X, in describing all of these possible pasts, is journeying back into various 'sheets of past', so that each of these descriptions are so many attempts for X to go back into the past, to seek out its layers and the relationships between those layers. As Bogue puts it:

> What Deleuze finds fascinating is that A seems to leap from peak to peak in a perpetual present, whereas X explores multiple sheets of the past, seeking out the 'brilliant points' of each memory space that might magnetically draw A into his story. Two conceptions of time coexist in the film, one of which Deleuze attributes primarily to Robbe-Grillet (peaks of the present), the other to Resnais (sheets of the past) (Bogue, 2003, p. 141).[1]

In *Last Year in Marienbad* not all of the events that are described could have happened – did X meet A in Marienbad or Friedrichsbad? Did X flee with A? Or did M kill A? To merely declare, however, that the sheets of past do not constitute a whole, that actual and virtual become indiscernible, or that we cannot definitively know what the distinction between the true and the false is, does not take us to the heart of *Last Year in Marienbad*. What Resnais is exploring is *how a memory can be made*. Such things happen to me very often, a friend or my wife will remark 'Don't you remember when we . . . ?' And suddenly a memory will come flooding back, the past will be opened up and be reborn, as though being brought back from the dead. *Last Year in Marienbad* is a meditation on such moments, as X asks A 'Don't you remember when we . . . ?' The film is nothing less than a great love story, for if X and A had an affair last year, then X wants A to remember it, and to make it a memory that is worth affirming. Against A's better wishes – for she should stay faithful to M (for we presume him to be her husband) – X effectively encourages A to revive a past that she is willing to renounce, just as the Japanese man in *Hiroshima, mon amour* encourages the French woman to recover her past from Nevers. With X's attempts to bring back the past, to open up the past – did this really happen, can we discover together what happened? – the virtual (past) comes into contact with the actual (present). This opening up of the virtual past, a virtual that is in a state of 'becoming', is what is utterly essential for the time-image, for it is an image of time in which the past can be rediscovered, reinvented, opened up and discovered anew. What this in turn means is that the future too can be opened up and subject to change: if A rediscovers this past that may or may not have happened 'last year in Marienbad', then she can finally renounce her relationship with M and embark on a new life with X. If X and A can discover a new past together, they can also forge a new future together. That is what is at stake for the time-image. Of course, A might well flee with X, or she might alternatively be shot dead by M. We cannot know. But these are the risks of creating a new past and a new future: we cannot know what the consequences will be.

We can find the same stakes of the past's relation to the future at play in *Mon oncle d'Amérique*. It is René who, at the end of the film, creates a new past for himself. He will now renounce his job with the textile firm and thus reinvent his past, start afresh and begin life anew (let us merely say that he will rediscover his love for his wife and family). By contrast, Jean will become more and more rigid, he will shore up his own stakes in the past (as signified by his quest to find his grandfather's papers) and use that rigidified past to shore up his own stakes in an unchanging future, to ensure his own privileges and place in the social hierarchy is maintained. We are, I hope, beginning to understand the full potential and importance of the time-image.

8

Thought and Cinema

What is thought, or what is thinking? Deleuze somewhat dramatically claims that the movement-image seems to reach a point at which thought fails it. He declares, for example, that, on the basis of the movement-image, 'Cinema is dying [. . .] from its quantitative mediocrity', and even that 'The spiritual automaton' – under the conditions of the movement-image – 'became fascist man' (Deleuze, 1989, p. 164). In other words, despite the grandeur and brilliance of the movement-image, especially in the hands of a filmmaker like Eisenstein, it nevertheless produced modes of thought that could be utilized by fascism, and a filmmaker like Leni Riefenstahl ('who was not mediocre', Deleuze assures us; ibid) was every bit as capable of producing brilliant movement-images as were Eisenstein, Gance, Hawks and others. Such, then, were the low points of the movement-image. What the time-image promised, therefore, in the wake of World War II and fascism, was the ability to put cinema back into contact with thought.

But what, after all, is thought? The best way to approach this question for Deleuze is to associate thought with judgement. For the movement-image, thinking is a matter of judgement, while for the time-image, thinking becomes a matter of refraining from judgement. One of the primary ways of distinguishing films of the movement-image from those of the time-image is that the former are determined and resolved typically by way of an ethical judgement: as a movement-image film progresses, we are made aware of how one should choose between good and evil, and we are convinced that siding with the good is a right and proper thing to do. In short, while watching a movement-image film, we become conscious of how to judge good actions over bad ones and good decisions over bad ones. Even when such decisions or actions are not entirely easy to make, as occurs, for example, in Kazan's *Wild River*, we are nevertheless still left with a sense that 'this is how things should be' or 'how things must be'; in *Wild River*, that the Tennessee Valley must be dammed in order to control its devastating yearly floods. For the movement-image, good must be distinguished from evil, just as the true will be clearly distinguished from the false, the real from the imaginary, the present from the past.

What about Hitchcock's films? Did Deleuze not argue that Hitchcock's films produced a 'mental image'; that they introduced relation-images based on thought? Might it be true that Hitchcock introduced a kind of thought to the movement-image that differs markedly from Eisenstein, Riefenstahl or Kazan? Hitchcock certainly introduced a different kind of thought to the movement-image, but this was not enough to take his films entirely in the direction of the time-image. The kinds of thoughts produced by Hitchcock's films are based on *interpretation* and *discovery*. That is, thinking in Hitchcock's films is based on weighing up the existing relations between things or discovering a true relation between things. Even if Guy Haines is put in a difficult position in *Strangers on a Train*, he still manages to use his intelligence and strength to ensure the truth of the matter is uncovered in the end (that he was framed by Bruno); and even if there are doubles which push into the territory of the time-image in *Vertigo*, Scottie, at the end of the film, nevertheless discovers the truth of his being duped, even if he has no idea what to do with this truth. His revenge at the end of the film is to have demonstrated that the true is also the good, to have shown to Judy that 'she shouldn't have been such a good liar', that doing good is always a better path to take than the path of evil, so that, at the end of the film, the punishment for evil is meted out by God at the mission of San Sebastian. We know, by the end of the film, how to judge which actions are good and which are evil and how to distinguish the truth from the lie. By contrast, in a film of the time-image like *Europa '51*, when Irene seeks her own truths, her society condemns her for it and refuses to recognize those truths as truths; it condemns them and incarcerates her. In such films, the status of the good and the true is put into question. Here, if the good and the true are subject to judgement, then those judgements become difficult to make, if not impossible. Judgement falters as a way of clearly distinguishing between good and evil, true and false.

What, therefore, is judgement? For Deleuze, judgement involves the invocation of a higher cause or higher authority. Essentially, to judge is to appeal to God or to the good as a higher authority. From Nietzsche, Deleuze asserts that judgement is 'the consciousness of being in debt to the deity' (Deleuze, 1998a, p. 126), which is to say that any judgement is made only on the basis of an appeal to a higher authority: one is told beforehand how to judge, and on the basis of having been told, one makes a judgement. Operations of judgement are central to films of the movement-image: for Griffith's *Birth of a Nation*, as much as for Ford's *Stagecoach* (where the criminal and the good-hearted prostitute define the terrain of a new America) and Kazan's *Wild River*. Judgement is found in Hawks too, for *The Big Sky* resolves itself in favour of 'free trade' and against the malicious trading practices of the rival firm, while *Gentlemen Prefer Blondes* invokes a court which judges beauty to be naturally allied with money. For the time-image, there are no such triumphs of judgement: Guido is not judged for his past misdemeanours in *8½*, Kane is not subject to judgement in *Citizen Kane*, while judgement is not even an issue for films like *Last Year in Marienbad* or *La ronde*.

As noted in the Introduction, Deleuze's understanding of thought in the *Cinema* books is guided by Spinoza's notion of a 'spiritual automaton', a notion which, for cinema, was expressed quite perfectly by Georges Duhamel's exclamation that 'I can no longer think what I want to think. My thoughts have been replaced by moving images' (see Deleuze, 1989, p. 166). For Deleuze, not being able to determine what I want to think is precisely where thinking begins from and one of the great tasks of the dream of cinema was to demonstrate to us that we are not masters of our own thoughts. Rather, thoughts have their own life, their own spirit – they are spiritual automata, machines of the spirit which are capable of generation and creation. Cinema is itself a machine of thought. The machine which generates thoughts in the movement-image is somewhat different from that which produces thoughts in the time-image. We shall see what the stakes of this difference are.

Eisenstein: A Shock to Thought

Eisenstein's films are positive proof that the movement-image is more than capable of producing great thoughts. Deleuze argues that it is none other than the movement essential to the movement-image that renders it capable of producing thought. The movements of cinema's images can produce their own effects on the world and on viewers. In short, viewers can be 'moved' to think by the movement-image.

Eisenstein takes this capacity for 'moving thought' further than any other auteur of the movement-image, for he takes movement in the direction of shock. And such is the formula Deleuze invokes for the thoughts promulgated by the movement-image: 'It is as if cinema were telling us: with me, with the movement-image, you can't escape the shock that arouses the thinker in you' (Deleuze, 1989, p. 156). It is thus primarily by engaging shock that thought comes into contact with the movement-image.

Deleuze also invokes the sublime with reference to Eisenstein, for as we saw in Chapter 2, the sublime entails raising humankind above its sins and deficiencies so that it might be brought into contact with a higher order of being (to read again with Deleuze, 'the sublime is engendered within us in such a way that it prepares for a higher finality' [Deleuze, 1984, p. 52]). The sublime, derived from Kant, is the product of a conflict between the imagination and reason, and it is this conflict which provides a 'shock to thought' appropriate for the movement-image.

Thus, alongside the mathematical sublime of Gance and the dynamic sublime of Lang's silent films, Deleuze claims that Eisenstein achieves a 'dialectical sublime'. Eisenstein achieves this sublime in three ways, and here we can take the dialectic in terms of its traditional triplicate: thesis–antithesis–synthesis. '[T]he first moment', Deleuze states, 'goes from the image to thought, from the percept to the concept' (Deleuze, 1989, p. 157). To put this another way: Eisenstein will do such things to his film images that those images will set off resonances or reverberations of thought. The images I perceive (the 'percept') are put together in such a way that they stimulate thought (the 'concept'). Given Eisensteinian montage, we should not see such formulas as being overly difficult to grasp, for what Deleuze is claiming here is merely something which goes to the heart of Eisenstein's practice of dialectical montage. The oppositional clash between (or within) shots produces a shock: 'the shock' writes Deleuze, 'has an effect on the spirit, it forces it to think' (Deleuze, 1989, p. 158). And thus we have a 'spiritual automaton' of dialectical montage. Deleuze adds that this is the cinema of the 'kino-fist' advocated by Eisenstein.

But how can such a thing actually occur? The clash between the worker and the manager in *Strike* alluded to in Chapter 2 is apposite again here: the *clash* between their images, carefully edited so as to ensure the separate images of worker and manager almost never appear in the same shot, but instead are shaped in such a way that their bodies and heads constantly crash into each other, perfectly illustrates how this clash of images produces a 'shock to thought': we see these images and the concept is clear; *the worker is being treated unfairly.* Or, at the end of the same film, the juxtaposition of the striking workers being shot down by the police which is intercut with scenes of an ox being slaughtered: *the workers are being slaughtered like animals.* Or Martha's magnificent dream in *The General Line* with its images of an exuberant fecundity which multiplies over and over again in productive abundance: *a cooperative will create a land of plenty.* Or on the Odessa Steps in *The Battleship Potemkin*, where the shock of the 'Suddenly!' interrupts the pleasant camaraderie between the classes of the townspeople mourning the dead sailor: *the Tsar oppresses not only the poor and the lower classes, he oppresses everyone.*

There might be nothing especially profound in the production of such concepts (and Deleuze knows all too well that the destiny of dialectical montage has been none other than that of advertising and information, that 'the spiritual automaton was in danger of becoming the dummy of every kind of propaganda' [Deleuze, 1989, p. 157]). But the second of the three moments of the dialectical sublime (the 'antithesis') demonstrates Eisenstein's genius. The second moment goes 'from the concept to the affect'. If, as a first move, there is a movement from percept to concept, there is now a kind of reversal from the concept which now goes back to the affect. We should be careful not to see these moments as 'stages', for the concept does not come first to only then be followed by the affect. Rather, as Deleuze explains, ' "intellectual cinema" has as correlate "sensory thought" or "emotional intelligence", and is worthless without it' (Deleuze, 1989, p. 159). The percept, concept and affect emerge simultaneously, and some of Eisenstein's greatest writings attest to this (Eisenstein, 1963, 1988a, 1988b). Indeed, the concept cannot be dissociated from the affect for Eisenstein, so that the injustices of *Strike* we have mentioned cannot be separated from the rage one feels in support of the worker or the sheer horror felt at the juxtaposition of the slain ox and slain workers. Likewise, the Odessa Steps sequence is not merely an intellectual exercise, but the occasion of horror and astonishment ('we jumped out of our seats'). Martha's dream in *The General Line* is also charged with the affective ecstasy produced by what Eisenstein referred to as that film's 'overtonal montages' (Eisenstein, 1988b). Even the supposedly 'intellectual' montage of *October* cannot be divorced from the waves of enthusiasm, the rising up of the people in support of the Bolsheviks, and the discrediting of the Provisional government, the Mensheviks and the 'death battalion'. Deleuze argues that Eisenstein, especially for Martha's dream in *The General Line*, 'develops a pathos-filled power of imagination which reaches the limits of the universe, an "orgy of sensory representations", a visual music which is like mass, fountains of cream, fountains of luminous water, spurting fires, zigzags forming numbers' (Deleuze, 1989, p. 159).

The third moment: if first of all there is the passage from percept to concept, and secondly a movement from concept to affect, then the third moment – the synthesis – is the combination and unification of these two. As Deleuze puts it, this third moment is the completed circuit, a circuit which goes from *the image to thought*, then from *thought back to the image*. Deleuze's point is that, from the perspective of the movement-image, there cannot be thought without an image, the thought does not exist without the image, and nor does any thought exist without the affect which returns it to the image. What this all adds up to for Deleuze is that 'In the sublime there is a sensory-motor unity of nature and man' (Deleuze, 1989, p. 162); what the movement-image necessitates is 'the unity of nature and man, of the individual and the mass' (ibid.). This, then, is the ultimate end of thinking in the movement-image: the unity of man and world in a sublime conception of cinema.

Godard: To Believe in this World

If Eisenstein's films produce spiritual automata, then these are automata fit for revolution. The problem which the movement-image came up against was, however, that the automata it produced were just as fit for *Triumph of the Will* (1935) as for *October*: both could be said to posit the unity of man and world in a sublime conception of cinema. Duhamel's classic statement, that 'My thoughts have been replaced by moving images' were certainly applicable to *October*, but they were also applicable for *Triumph of the Will*, and, perhaps even worse than this for Deleuze, was that a cinema of shock came to be replaced with a lesser cinema of violent representation, a cinema of cheap thrills (see Deleuze, 1989, p. 157). Deleuze thus pursues the spiritual automaton in another direction, in the direction of the time-image, and this gives rise to a quite extraordinary conception of cinema's relation to thinking. 'Here', writes Deleuze, 'the spiritual automaton has become the mummy, the dismantled, paralysed, petrified, frozen instance which testifies to the "impossibility of thinking that is thought"' (Deleuze, 1989, p. 166).

We might initially consider that becoming a petrified, paralysed mummy sounds like something to be thoroughly repudiated, but for Deleuze it opens the way to a new conception of thought. And if we consider the kinds of characters we have come across so far in our discussions of the time-image – Irene in *Europa' 51*, Lidia in *La Notte*, Giulietta in *Giulietta degli spiriti*, Lola Montes, René in *Mon oncle d'Amérique* – then these are characters who are dismantled and mummified to certain degrees. What, however, might it mean to affirm 'the impossibility of thought that is thinking', a formula Deleuze borrows from the French writer, Maurice Blanchot? More than anything, this approach to thinking means that *one cannot really be thinking if one knows what one is thinking*. Rather, *to really be thinking is to come across that which is unknown*, to come across something which is impossible to think. To then try to begin to think this impossibility is to truly begin to think.

Where the thoughts of the movement-image aim to define a sublime unity between man and world, a mode of thinking where the image is united with the concept, what the time-image conjures

up is a *suspension of the world*. This conception of cinema, claims
Deleuze, 'far from making thought visible, as Eisenstein wanted, [is]
on the contrary directed towards what does not let itself be thought
in thought, and equally to what does not let itself be seen in vision'
(these conceptions are taken from Schefer, 1980; see Deleuze, 1989,
p. 168). Where the movement-image aims to depict a higher truth
– the good, the sublime, the unity of man and world – the time-
image instead tends to shatter depiction itself. If we consider such
a situation in terms of modes of judgement, then films of the time-
image refrain from judgement. Again, if we consider Eisenstein's
montages as representative of the logic of the movement-image –
the worker is being treated unfairly (*Strike*); *a cooperative will create a
land of plenty* (*The General Line*); *the Tsar oppresses all classes* (*The
Battleship Potemkin*) – then this is still a mode of thought in which
judgements are made and justice is sought: good is affirmed over
and above evil. All of this changes for the time-image; there are no
such truths or higher invocations of the good:

. . . it is not in the name of a better or truer world that thought
captures the intolerable in this world, but, on the contrary, it is
because this world is intolerable that it can no longer think a world
or think itself. The intolerable is no longer serious injustice, but the
permanent state of daily banality. Man *is not himself* other than
the one in which he experiences the intolerable and feels himself
trapped (Deleuze, 1989, pp. 169–170).

This is the state of thought for the time-image, a state where
humankind realizes that the world has become intolerable, that the
only way to confront this intolerability is to disintegrate all thought,
to admit that one is trapped . . . and to begin again. We should thus
realize that the characters we have met in our discussions of the
time-image are profoundly positive, that the supposed disintegration
of characters such as Lidia (in *La Notte*), Giulietta (in *Giulietta degli
spiriti*), René (in *Mon oncle d'Amérique*) and so on, are journeys that
are thoroughly affirmative. René offers perhaps the most appropriate
example. For him, the world becomes so intolerable that the only
way out is death, and yet he returns from the dead, to begin again.
In the same film, by contrast, Jean, a character from a background

of privilege, clings to his privileges, to his heritage, to a marriage of convenience, and remains resistant to change and thus resistant to thought.

Deleuze takes Jean-Luc Godard's films as exemplars of the thoughts produced by the time-image. Like Eisenstein, there are three moments to this process of thought, though this process, unlike Eisenstein's for the movement-image, is no longer resolved by the dialectic. Deleuze summarizes what is at stake for the mode of thinking produced by the time-image:

> Thus modern cinema develops new relations with thought from three points of view: the obliteration of a whole or of a totalization of images, in favour of an outside which is inserted between them; the erasure of the internal monologue as whole of the film, in favour of a free indirect discourse and vision; the erasure of the unity of man and the world, in favour of a break which now leaves us with only a belief in this world (Deleuze, 1989, pp. 187–8).

First of all, then, in contrast with the synthesizing tendencies of the movement-image in which individual shots and images are combined into greater unities and totalities – the 'shock to thought' of Eisenstein's montages is always raised up to a higher unity – the time-image instead emphasizes the breakages between images; it focuses on that which divides one image from another. And no auteur has gone further in this regard than Godard, from the use of jump-cuts in *Breathless* (1960), through the use of placards and intertitles in *Vivre sa vie* (1962) and *Masculin Féminin* (1966), to jarring juxtapositions of sound and image in *A Woman is a Woman* (1961), *Bande à part* (1964), or *Weekend* (1967), through to the disintegration of narrative in *Pierrot le fou* (1965), *Two or Three Things I Know About Her* (1967), and the later films, such as *For Ever Mozart* (1996), *Helas pour moi* (1993) or *In Praise of Love* (2001), not to mention the abrasive uses of colour in *Le Mépris* (1963), *Made in USA* (1966) or *La Chinoise* (1967).

What is at stake for these Godardian experiments is a sense in which cinema breaks free from the world, so that the question of the image and of montage is no longer one of reconnecting with the world, as it was for the movement-image ('the unity of nature and man, of the individual and the mass'; Deleuze, 1989, p. 162). Against this bringing together of man and the world, Godard's breakages between the image and the world instead introduce the 'unthought' element. Deleuze explains this process in the following manner: 'in Godard's method, it is not a question of association. Given one image, another image has to be chosen which will introduce an interstice *between* the two. This is not an operation of association, but of differentiation' (Deleuze, 1989, p. 179). If the movement-image is predicated on a circuit that goes from the image to the concept and back to the image, that is, on the *association* between them, and by extension, by the connection between thought and nature, between man and the world, then what the time-image introduces are gaps and breakages between these associations: the image is dissociated from the world, thought breaks away from nature, man is divorced from the world. What the gap or interstice between images introduces is a 'something else', a something that cannot be reduced to being an emanation of the world or nature and which cannot be something which one will 'put together'. Perhaps this is nowhere more recognizable in Godard's films than in a relatively late one, *In Praise of Love*. An extraordinary amount of this film is given over to the black screen inserted between images, where the black interstice is precisely a matter of introducing a 'something else' that is irreducible to its surrounding images. It is this kind of method, explains Deleuze, which occurs 'in such a way that a difference of potential is established between the two, which will be productive of a third or of something new' (Deleuze, 1989, p. 178). The production of a third or of something new is no longer a dialectical synthesis which results in a productive unity, but something new produced by a disconnection, a something which comes from the 'outside', as Deleuze puts it.

These points are crucial for Deleuze's notion of the thought of the time-image, but we still have a way to go before we can work out precisely how these elements function in Godard's films. To read again with Deleuze:

We have seen that the power of thought gave way, then, to an unthought in thought, to an irrational proper to thought, a point of outside beyond the outside world, but capable of restoring our belief in the world. The question is no longer: does cinema give us the illusion of the world? But: how does cinema restore our belief in the world? (Deleuze, 1989, pp. 181–2)

With the movement-image, the synthesis of thought and the world amounts to what Deleuze calls a 'power of thought' which joins the thoughts of humankind with an image of the world. The time-image, on the other hand, disrupts thought to such a degree that thought is riven by an 'unthought' in thought, an 'impower' of thought, that shatters the relation between humankind and the world. And yet, Deleuze rekindles some faith in cinema's vocation: it can restore our belief in the world. How, we must ask, does all of this work?

If first of all the time-image inserts an interstice – an 'outside' – between images which evokes the unthought in thought, then secondly, it delivers a mode of 'free indirect discourse'. But what is meant by this 'free indirect'? If the movement-image is defined by drawing clear distinctions between that which is subjective and that which is objective, that is, between what a subject sees and thinks on the one hand, and what can be objectively verified on the other, then the time-image tends to fuse the subjective and the objective. We have already seen cases of this in our discussions the actual (objective) and the virtual (subjective), and the present (objective) and the past (subjective). By invoking the 'free indirect', however, Deleuze appeals more closely to the micro-structures of cinematic discourse, for the free indirect invokes neither a subjective nor an objective point of view, but a position that is both/neither subjective and/or objective (on these points see Bogue, 2003, pp. 72–3; Rodowick, 1997, pp. 61–2).

Let us focus on a concrete example: from the perspective of the movement-image, Martha's dream in *The General Line* is definitively subjective in so far as it is a dream and therefore incontrovertibly something 'inside her head'. This is a 'subjective discourse', the product of an 'interior monologue' that Deleuze points to in Eisenstein. But the challenge for this kind of subjective discourse in the movement-image is to test whether or not that subjective vision can be made objective. Therefore, Martha's dream of the cooperative's fecundity is echoed throughout the film in the objective sequences which grant truth to Martha's subjective dream: the milk-separator sequence, the sequence in which the cow and bull are married and consummate their union, and finally in the miraculous reproducing powers of the tractors at the film's conclusion. Thus Martha's subjective vision is transformed into a unity of human and the world, of human and nature, in a totalizing synthesis which grants truth to the 'power of thought' (that is, the power of thought expressed by Martha's dream). Such is the logic of the movement-image.

By contrast, the time-image emerges in the wonderful scenes of Charlotte (Macha Méril) in Godard's *A Married Woman* (1964) as she flicks through a women's magazine (*Elle*) while visiting the local public swimming pool. Throughout the film we have been introduced to Charlotte's obsessions with body image, from taking a magazine test to 'determine the perfect bust', to discussions with her housemaid (Mrs Céline) who has taken a breast enhancement serum from Peru (with results that her husband has adored), and repeated images of billboard posters advertising images of feminine perfection, right up the point where, at the pool, there are flickering photographic flashes, including many reversals into negative exposure, of the 'skinny' girls who are bathing. So Charlotte flicks through the magazine images, page after page of underwear advertisements, images of women with perfect bodies and breasts, one after the other, again and again. The magazine images are, on the one hand, just like those dream images of Martha's in *The General Line*: images of the world being presented to an individual's dream-gaze; these are, for Charlotte, wish-images or dream-images. And yet these images or visions are no longer those of a subject, but instead are objective ones, published in a magazine. We are no longer certain where the subjective virtual ends – is Charlotte merely imagining, fantasizing, or dreaming these images? – and where the objective actual begins. And even more than this: Godard overlays these advertising images with a conversation between two young women at a nearby table as they discuss the pros and cons of topless bathing suits, and further emphasizes the disjunctive connections when a customer puts a pop song on the jukebox, a love song about a woman who spots her lover with another woman while at the cinema (and later in the film Charlotte will meet her lover in the cinema).

We might see Charlotte's state here as one of confusion: what do I want? What are my thoughts? What is subjective and what is objective? It is this disconnection between images and thoughts, the world and thought, nature and humankind that goes to the heart of Godard's discourse, according to Deleuze. It is a discourse which emphasizes the free indirect mode, so that the time-image no longer presents us with subjective image-thoughts which aspire to objectivity, but instead presents us with a collapsing of the distinction between the objective and the subjective. The interior monologue is externalized so that it is no longer the coming true of a subjective thought in a higher objective good that is at stake (as it was for Eisenstein, but no less for the other examples of the movement-image we have seen in Kazan, Gance, or Hawks and so on). Rather, for the time-image what is at stake is the evacuation of judgement, of the good, of thought itself, in the hope that, by dismantling or emptying thought and its associated judgements of the good, new thoughts can be born. This is what is at stake for the thoughts of the time-image.

Belief in this World

We have isolated two points at which the thought of the time-image differs from that of the movement-image: the unthought in thought which is produced by a dissociation between images, and the privileging of free indirect discourse. The third point Deleuze articulates is that the time-image no longer gives us an illusion of the world but instead advocates a restoration of *belief in this world*. What can Deleuze mean by such a declaration? Thankfully, we do not need to look very far to find answers. In the films of the time-image we have discussed, what is at stake is a dismantling of the world as it has been known and the rebirth (or at the very least an attempt at a rebirth) of the human's relation to the world. Irene in *Europe '51* breaks with the middle-class expectations of the world she has known and she gives birth to a new relation to the world (based on her attempts to help others), and we might make much the same kinds of claims from Guido in *8½*, Giulietta in *Giulietta degli spiriti*, René in *Mon oncle d'Amérique*, even perhaps of X and A in *Last Year in Marienbad* who attempt to construct a new past together on the basis of which they might find it possible to flee into a new future. All these characters, Deleuze implies, are looking for a new kind of belief. More than these examples, however, *Blow Up* might offer the most pointed example: at the end of the film, as we have already noted, the link between the man (the photographer) and the world (the photographs of the murdered body) has been severed; they are relics, images, illusions of a world that can no longer be known. But when the photographer stumbles inadvertently on the tennis playing mimes and picks up their imaginary tennis ball, then one can declare that a belief in this world has suddenly been affirmed for him. This is not a world based on knowledge or even on what is being seen – for there is no tennis ball there and we know it as much as the photographer does. It is, instead, the creation of a world based on belief – a mutual belief in this tennis ball being in this world. After that, we can indeed hear that imagined ball bounce: a new creation of the world.

For Godard, a re-ignition of this belief in the world is central. If he becomes more and disillusioned with cinema during the 1960s – from the invocation of the Lumières's 'Cinema is an invention without a future' in *Le Mépris* up to *Weekend*'s closing title announcing the 'End of cinema' – to the point where he more or less abandons it during the 1970s, then there is little question that a reborn faith in cinema occurs in the 1980s, beginning with his 'second first film', *Sauve qui peut (la vie)* (1980). It is as though, with this film and some of the ones that follow (*Passion* [1982], *Prénom Carmen* [1983], *Je vous salue, Marie* [1985]), Godard finds a new beauty in the world, so where in the 1960s we might have found blank interstices (*A Married Woman*) or abrasive juxtapositions (*Weekend*, for example), we now find an uncharted landscape; 'transitional shots' perhaps, in the sense given to them by Yasujiro Ozu, rather than 'gaps'. 'In the films of the early eighties', one writer claims, 'Godard is seeking nothing less than *a new way of seeing*' (Morrey, 2005, p. 135). The later films are contemplative and reflective rather than angry and irreverent. They are *reverent* films, might be one way of putting it. Godard's later films give a new ability to the image: no longer is the image only there as a mode of questioning or even critique, as a way of blasting apart the 'society of the spectacle'. Rather, cinema's images can also reveal the world to us – *this world*.

Je vous salue, Marie might even be the key film here, where against all the odds one is encouraged to believe. And instead of abrasive juxtapositions, Godard uses evocative transitional shots, typically of the setting sun, of the moon or of flowers in bloom (Jacques Aumont goes so far as to label these films – *Je vous salue, Marie*, *Prénom Carmen*, *Passion* and *Sauve qui peut*, as offering 'a new apprenticeship of the gaze'; Aumont, 1989, p. 238; quoted in Morrey 2005, p. 135). These are in one sense visions of Heaven, which is upheld as a beacon of belief, but they are also visions of *this* world, of this world's beauty, its promises and its life. There are two key scenes in the film. The first, that of Marie's 'holy communion' in which she struggles, wriggles and writhes in her bed while questioning what is happening to her and her body as a consequence of her miraculous virgin pregnancy. This is a cinematic masterclass in searching for *something* – for life, for spirit, for the attempt to willingly accept that which entered her from the outside. Godard suggested that he was inspired by Françoise Dolto's book, *The Gospel at the Risk of Psychoanalysis*, and the guiding argument there that 'thought may be fecundated by an idea, coming from elsewhere, without knowing who gave it to us' (see Sterritt, 1999, p. 175).

The shots of the scene are edited in a discontinuous fashion – with jump-cuts that hearken back to the rustling sheets of *Breathless* – so that sometimes Marie is naked, at other times she wears underclothes, while additionally the light shifts from daylight to dark night in no apparent order. Alain Bergala describes the logic of the sequence in the following way: 'These are *attempts at images*. Godard doesn't accumulate them, but erases them as he goes along, each one replacing the last, as though none of them were quite good enough' (Bergala, 1999, p. 51, quoted in Morrey, 2005, p. 137). What is offered is a startling provocation to cinematic thought in which the scene gestures towards making connections, putting things together, but without *synthesizing* those connections in the dialectical manner typical of Eisenstein and the movement-image. Rather, here, with the time-image, the images must be held together by something else, by the kind of link which Deleuze will call 'belief'.[1] We might summarize belief as: that thought which comes from the outside and which shatters us and the world as it has been given to us in order that we can rediscover *this* world. 'What we most lack is a belief in the world', Deleuze writes, 'we've quite lost the world, it's been taken from us. If you believe in the world you precipitate events, you engender new space-times, however small their surface or volume. It's what you call *Pietas*' (Deleuze, 1995, p. 176). Marie's stormy night of holy communion: a *pietas* that offers belief in this world.

The other key scene is that of Joseph's 'lesson'. If Mary's communion with the Holy Spirit constitutes one aspect of the film – that of the relationship between the human and the divine – then its other aspect is constituted by the entangled romantic relationships the film exposes, beginning with the separation of the married couple in Miéville's companion piece, *The Book of Mary*. One commentator contends that the project of *Je vous salue, Marie* is centred on the question of 'how to film love?' (Le Roux, 1985, p. 13, quoted in Morrey 2005, p. 136). If Mary's love of God is a heavenly gesture – a matter of *pietas* – then the very human loves of the various characters are earthly ones, gestures that unambiguously beckon us towards *this* world. The squabbles, problems, conversations and arguments of those in and out of love are a cornerstone of Godard's films from the beginning (we have already seen this in *A Married Woman*, for example) so that a belief in this world is, for *Je vous salue, Marie* as much as any of the other films, about learning acts of love and trust. That is one way to discover a belief in this world. In the key scene of Joseph's lesson, he at first repeatedly declares to Marie, 'I love you' while touching her on her pregnant belly. But Marie repudiates him with continuous shouts of 'No!' After the intervention of the Angel Gabriel who brutally advises Joseph to sacrifice himself (that is, to sacrifice his carnal wishes), Joseph returns to his declarations of love for Marie, and this time she approves: 'Oui, oui, oui'. One scholar describes this change as one in which Joseph learns that 'to say "I love you" is not about getting one's hands on, but about letting go' (Nettlebeck, 2001, p. 91, quoted in Morrey 2005, p. 136). Contrary to an ethics of ownership, domination, and action – of winning someone's love in the way that Lorelei, for example, wins the love of Gus in *Gentlemen Prefer Blondes*, or the way that Terry decisively wins the love of Edie in *On the Waterfront* – here love is won by a process of letting go, of refraining from forcing one's hopes, desires and thoughts on another, but rather letting the thought of the outside take its own course, to acknowledge that one is not yet thinking. Such are the thoughts of the time-image.

Some of Deleuze's later essays provide ways of properly understanding what he is getting at when he writes about the thought of the outside and the 'impower' of thought. Deleuze is adamant, for example, that thinking cannot be modelled on notions of communication:

> Primarily, communication is the transmission and propagation of information. What is information? [. . .] Information is a set of imperatives, slogans, directions – order-words. When you are informed, you are told what you are supposed to believe. In other words, informing means circulating an order-word. Police declarations are appropriately called communiqués. Information is communicated to us, they tell us what we are supposed to be ready to, or have to, or be held to believe. And not even believe, but pretend like we believe. We are not asked to believe but to behave as if we did. This is information, communication (Deleuze, 2006, pp. 320–1).

What Deleuze is explaining here is a regime of *being told what to believe*, and he is opposed to such a version of feigned belief in no uncertain terms. Against such a regime, to *really* believe in this world is to resist at all costs what one is told to believe (and thus to refuse what one is told about divisions between good and evil, the true and the false, the actual and the virtual, and so on). And that is the lesson to be taken from Godard's films, from beginning to end: that they refuse to teach us anything, to tell us anything, to preach to us or give us lessons. What we have to do with them is find our own paths towards discovering a belief in this world.

9

Cinema After Deleuze (I): The Persistence of the Movement-Image

Writing in the 1980s, after a breathtaking twenty years or more in the history of cinema – the new waves and the 1960s and the rise of a so-called 'New Hollywood' in the 1970s – Deleuze might have hoped that films of the time-image would eventually come to replace those of the movement-image and that cinema would be at the forefront of exhibiting a new mode of thought (as discussed in Chapter 8). No such thing has occurred: today, as in the past, far more movement-image films are made than time-image films. But we should not see such an outcome as demonstrating a flaw in Deleuze's grand classification of cinema. First of all, Deleuze never tries to argue that the time-image is necessarily an improvement, in a progressive sense, of the movement-image. Historically, therefore, we should not come to think that the time-image 'follows' the movement-image in a way that would make the movement-image obsolete or redundant, as though it might die off. And secondly, Deleuze argues that the time-image was always 'implicit' in the movement-image, so that it is correct to declare that the time-image is merely downplayed in the films of the movement-image. And so too for the time-image: the movement-image is implicit there, so that we can say the history of cinema from Deleuze's perspective presents us with a constant to-ing and fro-ing between the movement-image and time-image. This back and forth constitutes the great semiotic division in Deleuze's classification of cinema.

Might cinema be capable of producing other images? Might there have emerged another grand semiotic division since Deleuze wrote his books, for example, a 'digital-image' or 'silicon-image'? Perhaps. But I am of the opinion that much of Deleuze's grand division between the movement-image and the time-image is still capable of accounting for the bulk of cinematic production, though admittedly I might be at a loss to describe where short 'internet films' or contemporary 'gallery films' might fit in to Deleuze's semiotic. In this chapter and the one that follows, therefore, I concentrate on feature films produced in the last thirty years or so to try to pick out some notable elements of the movement-image and the time-image during that period.

Steven Spielberg: Echoes of the Large Form

Deleuze ignores the two most successful films of the second half of the 1970s – *Jaws* (1975) and *Star Wars* (1977) – for it is these two films which seem to signal the end of a potentially 'new' Hollywood, while also hailing the beginning of another new kind of Hollywood based on the 'blockbuster'. I cannot help thinking Deleuze might have been very specifically thinking of *Jaws* and *Star Wars* when he declared that 'Cinema is dying [. . .] from its quantitative mediocrity' (Deleuze, 1989, p. 164), that cinema had 'drowned in the nullity of its productions' (ibid.) and that the shockingly great montages of Eisenstein are now merely replicated as 'violent representations'. A case against a film like *Jaws* developed along these lines might well be possible from a Deleuzian perspective. However, a distance of more than thirty years, especially given the extraordinary success and influence of a filmmaker like Steven Spielberg, director of *Jaws* (I take up the influence of *Star Wars* later in this chapter), might present us today with a markedly different set of observations. Against Deleuze's own provocations of mediocrity and nullity we should affirm the Deleuze who declares that 'the cinema is always as perfect as it can be' (Deleuze, 1986, p. x). Or another way of approaching this issue is simply to assert that, if Deleuze were writing the *Cinema* books today, there is no way he could ignore the contribution of Spielberg.

What, then, does Spielberg do to cinema? The short answer is: he restores the grandeur of the large form of the action-image. If the large form had come under increasing pressure during the 1950s and 1960s in American cinema – as we have seen with filmmakers like Kazan, Hawks and Hitchcock – then Spielberg unashamedly restores its force and influence. And if the large form of the action-image had at its core the triumph of the American dream, which was also a triumph of American cinema, then Spielberg gives new life to this cinematic dream. And yet, at the same time, this dream has changed profoundly. It is no longer the dream of founding a great civilization, as it was with Ford, and nor is it a dream of founding a great ethical society, as it was with Kazan. Spielberg composes cinematic dreams which are quite different from those of the classical large form. Gone is the dream of the grand nation or the great society. What is left are small dreams, dreamt only by individuals or small familial groups. That is Spielberg's definitive contribution: to have erased the American dream that might ever have been based on community or a New Deal and to have replaced it with a dream where every man or woman must strive to find his or her own personal dreamland.

The Spielberg hero is typically a loner in some sense – certainly in *Duel* (1971), and perhaps most forcefully in *Close Encounters of the Third Kind* (1977) and also in *E.T.* (1982), the *Indiana Jones* movies (1981, 1984, 1989, 2008) and in more recent films like *Catch Me If You Can* (2002), *The Terminal* (2004) and *Minority Report* (2002). All of these films are about an individual's battles with an 'evil empire' of one sort or another, from the Nazi caricatures of *Indiana Jones* to the 'real' Nazis of *Saving Private Ryan* (1998) and *Schindler's List* (1993), through the technical and bureaucratic experts of *Close Encounters of the Third Kind*, *E.T.* and *The Terminal* or the governmental conspirators of *Minority Report*. Unlike the classic films of the large form, none of these films is overtly about the ethical founding of a new community or civilization – gone are the ethical imperatives of *On the Waterfront* or *Sergeant Rutledge*. In some ways, Spielberg retains some aspects of the small form in as much as his heroes typically escape with their lives and there is little sense in the films of the founding of a new America. However, Spielberg usually presents a vision of middle-class America, that is, in one way or another, on the verge of falling apart, a point best exploited in *Jurassic Park's* (1993) vision of the capitalist theme park gone awry and the compromised dreams of the small holiday town in *Jaws*, with grander versions of a disintegrating world being offered in *Schindler's List* or *War of the Worlds* (2005) and *Minority Report*.

Spielberg sticks very closely to the SAS' format of the large form, to the designation of 'modes of behaviour', to the need for action from the hero, which typically leads to a final duel in which a new stable situation is found. These very traditional modes of storytelling in the cinema are affirmed by Spielberg's films. The vision of the 'ethical' is, however, where these films distinguish themselves from the large form films of the classical type that we have seen in Ford and Kazan. One commentator has defined a set of three ethical commandments to which Spielberg's plots adhere: 1) never abandon the family; 2) never place public advancement above personal loyalty; and 3) never sacrifice ethical principles for the supposed good of the many (Friedman, 2006, pp. 35–6). Gone then is the whole dynamic of the ethical division of the classical large form where Terry Malloy (in *On the Waterfront*) must go against the mob 'family' and forego personal loyalty (to his brother, to Johnny Friendly) in order to provide an ethical foundation in which 'the good of the many' is affirmed. And even more so in Kazan's *Wild River* is the notion of the family and personal loyalty put in question in the name of the ethical advancement of the many as one older vision of America is replaced with the egalitarian promises of the New Deal. None of this survives in Spielberg.

What takes the place of the ethical vision of the classical version of the large form is what might be referred to as a 'late capitalist' ethics. As argued brilliantly by Fredric Jameson (in an article published in 1979, before Deleuze had written the *Cinema* books), the turning point is *Jaws*, and few commentators today would argue with the fact that *Jaws* is a turning point in the history of cinema. Jameson tries to discern the social and political reasons why *Jaws* struck such a chord. And he successfully argues that *Jaws* pinpoints the division between an older America – perhaps the one of Ford and Kazan – and a new America. In *Jaws*, Quint, the old-time fisherman, on whose boat the monstrous shark is tracked down, represents, claims Jameson, 'the America of small business and individual private enterprise of a now outmoded kind, but also the America of the New Deal and the crusade against Nazism, the older America of the depression and the war and of the heyday of classical liberalism' (Jameson, 1992, p. 38). Quint, of course, is the one of the three hunters who dies in the final duel with the shark (a death which does not occur in the novel on which the movie is based), while the younger figures, the figures of a New America – the policeman Brody and Hooper the scientist – survive. Their survival is crucial for Jameson's analysis:

> [T]he content of the partnership between Hooper and Brody projected by the film may be specified socially and politically, as the allegory of an alliance between the forces of law-and-order and the new technocracy of the multinational corporations, an alliance which must be cemented, not merely by its fantasized triumph over the ill-defined menace of the shark itself, but above all by the indispensable effacement of that more traditional image of an older America which must be eliminated from historical consciousness and social memory before the new power system takes its place (Jameson, 1992, p. 38).

In Spielberg's hands, the large form finds itself adapted to an ethics of late capitalist America. Erased is the specific nature of the American dream that had so strongly figured in the history of the American cinema since Griffith through so many rebirths of a nation. Replacing it is a dislocated mélange of individuals and disconnected tribes, overshadowed by multinational technocracies which are beyond any individual's understanding or control. Such a new order is perfectly aligned with Spielberg's masterful control over special effects, lens manipulation, camera movement and rapid editing – all elements of what David Bordwell has called a style of 'intensive continuity' dominant in American cinema since the 1980s (see Bordwell, 2002; cf. Buckland, 2006).

A key image and technique is the zoom-in combined with tracking-out shots from *Jaws*, when Brody feels he has spotted the shark. As is well known, the technique is borrowed from Hitchcock's *Vertigo*, but it has a different effect there from the one it has in *Jaws*. For *Vertigo*, the 'vertigo effect' is one which externalizes Scottie's acrophobia; it gives us, as viewers, a sense of 'what it feels like' – the affection-image, par excellence; the material sensation of a neurological tic. The effect in *Jaws* provides the exact opposite, for rather than externalizing a feeling, its effect is one of intense *internalization* (see Buckland, 2006, p. 99). The consequences of this are central for Spielberg's aesthetic: no longer is the 'interior monologue' of the movement-image, one in which the dream of an individual might have the chance to be universalized, as in Martha's dream of the cooperative in Eisenstein's *The General Line*, as much as it occurs for Terry Malloy or even for Lorelei in *Gentlemen Prefer Blondes*, a film that promotes the dream of marriage as a universal principle. In other words, for Spielberg there is no longer a sense in which a subjective dream might be made objective. Rather, for Spielberg there is no universalization other than the universalization of isolated individuality. This situation is one which the zoom-in/track-out shot aestheticizes with precision: the intense internalization and personalization of a feeling, a feeling of being alone in the world, of being overawed by the world where it is impossible to obtain a public, communal consensus about what the world is, or any sense of what is at stake in that world. From one perspective, all Spielberg's works are usually concerned with the destiny of the individual in a world or society which has abandoned him (or, very occasionally, her – in *The Color Purple* [1985]): David Mann in *Duel*, Brody in *Jaws*, Roy Neary in *Close Encounters of the Third Kind*, Jones in the *Indiana Jones* films, Elliott in *E.T.*, the destiny and choices made by Schindler in *Schindler's List*, and so on. If the heroes of these films are cast adrift, however, they never suffer the kinds of crises of action we find in films of the time-image (in Rossellini, Antonioni and Resnais). The heroes of these films are never totally cast adrift, never reduced to a degree zero, for they always manage to find ways of reconnecting with the world – for Spielberg there can be no unhappy endings.

From another perspective, for Spielberg, alongside an ethics of the isolated individual there is also an ethics of the family. The family is rarely 'natural' in these films. Rather, it always begins as dismembered in one way or another and needs to be (re-)constituted. The clearest example of this ethic is the makeshift family of *Jurassic Park*, where Alan (Sam Neill) is assured by the end of the film of the virtues of family life against the backdrop of worldly (capitalist) pursuits, to never place personal advancement or the supposed common good above the family (and the family ethic is, for Spielberg, intrinsically good). 'Spielberg's movies', writes one scholar, 'consistently revolve around the formation of makeshift or ad hoc surrogate families banding together to defeat some common enemy' (Friedman, 2006, p. 285).

Many of these points come together in *Minority Report*, a fine example of the contemporary movement-image. This film is based on the notion of 'pre-crime': there are three gifted 'seers' who have visions of future crimes, and interpreting the visions of these seers allows the police force in a Washington D.C. of the future to solve crimes before they happen. The police department's chief 'pre-crime' analyst, John Anderton (Tom Cruise), an expert in solving these 'pre-crimes', is himself implicated in a murder (we can immediately see the link with Vargas in Welles' *Touch of Evil* here). Anderton thus becomes the object of a massive police hunt. In order to prove his innocence, and further to prove that he has been framed, he abducts the most gifted of the 'seers' – called 'pre-cogs' because of their ability to foretell events. Anderton does this for two reasons. First, this pre-cog can allow him to see his own future and enable him to stay one step ahead of his pursuers. Second, there is a hidden crime that is the key to Anderton's dilemma: this pre-cog's visions provide the sole piece of evidence of a crime committed some years ago by the head of the pre-crime unit, Lamar Burgess (Max von Sydow) – he had murdered none other than the mother of the pre-cog Anderton has abducted (no need to point out that this was a crime against the family unit carried out in the name of a higher cause, for the supposed 'good of the many'). When Burgess's crime is exposed, Anderton's innocence is thus proven and at the end of the film he is reunited with his wife – who additionally is now expecting their unborn son: the sanctity of the family again triumphs, just as much as the singular fight of the individual triumphs over a bureaucratic society.

Might we therefore see this film as demonstrating an ethics of the good against the evil combination of law and order and multinational capital? Are we not thus a long way from *Jaws* and its supposed advocacy of that combination? Well . . . no. It is important to discern just where *Minority Report*'s critique lies. The film demonstrates that the notion of seeing the future – by way of the gifted pre-cogs who predict crimes – is not in itself flawed. The film does not criticize this notion of being able to predict the future and then change the present on the basis of that prediction – indeed, it is an essential part of Anderton's success in avoiding being caught by the police and is also useful when Anderton faces the final duel with Burgess. Rather, the flaw in the system is a human one: such a gift of being able to see into the future cannot be entrusted to communal forces or social orders like governments or justice systems, for attempts to build societies according to such grand organizational principles are doomed to failure, for there will always be a Stalin or a Hitler (or even a George W. Bush and his Department of Homeland Security) which will push such organizations towards disaster. The attempt to form such collectives – a mainstay of the classical movement-image – is discredited in *Minority Report* (and is an essential component of all of Spielberg's films). In the hands of the individual, on the contrary, the ability to see the future is an inherently good thing. The film's opposition is therefore between the abilities of the collective will in late capitalist society and that of the individual will. The individual will is here inherently good, while the collective will is evil. (It is worth pointing out how such a perspective suits the ideals of late capitalism and that the reuniting of Anderton with his wife at the end of the film is much the same as the uniting of Brody and Hooper at the end of *Jaws* as they paddle back to Amity on the wreckage of the 'Orca'.)

The connections *Minority Report* makes between the future, the present and the past also unambiguously make it a movement-image film: to be able to predict the future means we will not only be able to fix the present (and solve crimes, for example, before they are committed), but it also means we will be able to fix the past. Not only is the 'truth' of the past restored when Burgess is discovered to be the murderer of the mother of the pre-cog, but this exposure also allows John Anderton to overcome his own demons from the past: the death of his young son some years ago had left him psychologically distraught and had caused his separation from his wife. All of this is put in perspective at the end of the film, however, when he is reunited with his wife and it is clear they are expecting another child. Now, the past, the present and the future are in their rightful place. There should be no need to point out that such a perspective on the past is a central concern for Spielberg: the truth of the past must be revealed for us so that it can teach us how to live in the present and the future, whether this concerns the Holocaust (*Schindler's List*), World War II (*Saving Private Ryan*), the comic-mythical pasts of the *Indiana Jones* films, or the history of slavery in the U.S. (*The Color Purple*, *Amistad* [1997]). No auteur has done more since the 1970s to resuscitate the movement-image in American cinema.

Martin Scorsese: Picking up the Pieces of the Small Form

If Spielberg shows us the reinvention of the American dream, albeit in ways that differ markedly from the classical large form of that dream, then Martin Scorsese repeatedly shows us how that dream continues to go drastically wrong. Deleuze himself more or less foresees this direction in American cinema when, at the end of the *Cinema 1*, he concentrates on the 'crisis' of the movement-image. During the late 1960s and 1970s, some elements of American cinema stepped decisively away from the movement-image even if they did not thereby land upon the shores of the time-image. Deleuze carefully goes through five points which defined this new style in Hollywood:

1. Situations are no longer as fixed as they once were; rather, they are 'dispersive'. In other words, they no longer begin from a set place and head in a set direction but instead begin from any number of disjointed places and head in directions that are ill-defined.

2. Connections between situations and actions are now thin, loose or vague; there is no easy or set way to get from S→A or vice versa. Characters also lose their abilities to act in self-defined ways and are instead 'acted upon' or they seem to 'undergo' action. Deleuze cites the end of Scorsese's *Taxi Driver* (1976) as an example here, for at the end of the film, it is as though Travis Bickle

(Robert DeNiro) is no longer capable of motivating his own actions, but instead carries out the series of bloody shootings as though it were a dream or as if he were in some sort of trance. This is no longer the kind of decisiveness we might expect from a Ringo Kid or a Terry Malloy.

3. Sensory-motor action has been replaced by a kind of 'wandering', a journey that lacks a specific destination. Again *Taxi Driver* provides a good example here (what does Travis want, where is he going?), though *Easy Rider* (1969) and the rise of the road movie provide key examples for Deleuze.

4. Narrative is worn out, for there are no new stories to tell. This is in effect what Deleuze is declaring when he writes 'Nothing but clichés, clichés everywhere . . . ' (Deleuze, 1986, p. 208). Stories of American triumph or even of those where a hero merely saves his own skin (as in examples of the 'small form') no longer work or are no longer relevant. They are replaced by shards of stories we seem to have heard before – gangsters in *The Godfather* (1972), cowboys in Peckinpah or Altman (*McCabe and Mrs Miller* [1971], *Buffalo Bill and the Indians, or Sitting Bull's History Lesson* [1976], even *Nashville* [1975]), the fight for justice and freedom in Lumet's *Serpico* (1973), *Dog Day Afternoon* (1976) or *The Verdict* (1982). These are stories which fail to have the kinds of endings in which an ethics of the good is asserted (as would traditionally be expected of movement-image films).

5. The 'organization of misery', a phrase Deleuze borrows from the romantic poet, William Blake. Deleuze takes this as a definitive end to the American dream of the type seen in the large form of the action-image. Now that the dream is over, the grand organization of any kind of communal world order can only ever be miserable, and this is something we have already seen at play in Spielberg's films. Its beginnings can be located in films like *The Manchurian Candidate* and John Ford's *The Man Who Shot Liberty Valance* – both made in 1962 during the Kennedy presidency – where a suspicion of power and what it means to govern come under severe pressure. By the time we get to films like Lumet's *The Anderson Tapes* (1971) or *Network* (1976), Coppola's *The Conversation* (1974), the Vietnam War, *All The President's Men*

(1976) and the Watergate Scandal itself, then a whole 'organization of misery' is put in place. All of Scorsese's films are about this: the organization of misery.

Fredric Jameson again provides a starting point here, for it is with Coppola's *The Godfather* that this 'organization of misery' comes to the fore. Jameson's diagnosis is bold: that the organization of misery is nothing but the organization of post-war corporate capitalism in America. He argues that with films like *The Godfather*, this post-war political and economic organization is deflected onto or distorted by the pure evil of the Mafia family – an operation of ideology, no less. As a result, what should be an issue of politico-economic organization, for Jameson, is transformed into an issue of the ethics of the evil Mafia family. The message of films like *The Godfather* is, therefore, that the problems of post-war America are not to be blamed on a capitalist 'organization of misery' but are instead the result of corruption and evil. Jameson writes: 'Mafia films thus project a "solution" to social contradictions – incorruptibility, honesty, crime fighting and finally law-and-order itself – which is evidently a very different proposition from that diagnosis of the American misery whose prescription would be social revolution' (Jameson, 1992, p. 43). Long gone are the days when rattin' on the mob might lead to a social revolution in miniature (*On the Waterfront*) or where government intervention itself might herald social revolution (*Wild River*), but also gone are the days when a hero at the edge of the law will refound justice on the basis of a new order (*Stagecoach*, *Sergeant Rutledge*). What we are left with is an ethical commandment to rid the world of evil, but with absolutely no idea of how this might be done; that is, a belief that the social order is corrupt to the core – and intolerable, as Antonioni, Godard or Resnais showed from the perspective of the time-image – but with no sense of how to get out of that mess. All we can do is endlessly reproduce and replay this 'organization of misery'.

Scorsese's films extend and complicate this diagnosis by showing us how closely linked the worlds of the Mafia 'family business' and American corporate capitalism are, from the pimps of *Taxi Driver* to the gangster worlds of *Mean Streets* (1973), *Goodfellas* (1990) and *Casino* (1995), or the professional boxing excesses of *Raging*

Bull (1980), from the pool hustlers of *The Color of Money* (1986) to the Irish gangsters of *Gangs of New York* (2002) and *The Departed* (2006), and even in the compromised lawyer of *Cape Fear* (1991) or the embittered small-time entertainer of *King of Comedy* (1982). For Scorsese, these are so many arms or guises of capitalist corruption that have enforced nothing less than an organization of misery on America. It is no longer the Mafia family as distinct from corporate capitalism of the kind found in *The Godfather*. Rather, the problem for Scorsese is that it is not possible to tell the difference anymore between the supposedly evil Mafia family and the seemingly good capitalist, for it is as though these roles have all fused into one great mélange of evil which produces and sustains the organization of misery. There is no longer the good capitalist, such as the generous and fair old man in *Gentlemen Prefer Blondes* who can be distinguished from the swindler Beekman who is merely a crook, and nor do we have the division between good free market trading and the corrupted forces of evil trading (we can easily call them gangsters) one finds in *The Big Sky*. Rather, now the swindler is the same as the generous gentleman, and the corrupt forces of the Mafia hitmen are the ones who define trade per se. Not even the forces of law and order can be distinguished from the simmering pot of evil (as made explicit in recent films like *Gangs of New York*, *The Departed* and *Shutter Island* [2010]). Such is Scorsese's 'organization of misery'.

Broadly speaking, following in the footsteps of someone like Hawks, Scorsese stays true to the small form – ASA' – where the action stumbles from one situation to another with no clear direction. There is a sense of haphazardness here, in which characters find things along the way to add to the collections which make up their lives. We see this in Travis Bickle's encounters with the prostitute or the politician in *Taxi Driver*; in Eddie Nelson's (Paul Newman) discovery of a protegé whom he takes on a journey into a world of hustler capitalism in *The Color of Money*. We see it in Sam Rothstein (Robert DeNiro) in *Casino* as he stumbles into the casino racket, falls in love and confronts a series of problems that arise. Likewise for the police chief (Alec Baldwin) in *The Departed* who pieces together groupings and strategies on the spur of the moment, not to mention the reactions to these actions needed by the corrupt cop (Matt Damon) and the undercover cop (Leonardo DiCaprio). Here, as is typical of the small form, there are always actions (A) which result in a number of situations (S) which then require further actions (A'). The driving force for the central characters in these films is the need to always stay 'one step ahead', to anticipate the situation and the action which will be required in answer to that situation, to always foresee a reaction that will be sufficient for a situation to come. This is a storytelling strategy Scorsese exploits throughout his career (it can be found in *Mean Streets* and *Goodfellas* as much as in *The Color of Money* or *Shutter Island*).

It is perhaps in *Casino* where these conflicts and strategies find their clearest expression. A middle-management Mafia figure, Sam Rothstein, is sent to Las Vegas by the Mafia overlords in order to oversee the operations of a casino. The casino is portrayed by Scorsese as the capitalist venture par excellence, where customers more or less willingly give away their money, where the house always wins, where money is conveniently syphoned off and sent back to the mob bosses back East, and all the while the State's senators, regulators and sheriffs are kept happy with kickbacks, gifts and sweet deals. Here, Fredric Jameson's negative vision of 'an alliance between the forces of law-and-order and the new technocracy of the multinational corporations' no longer needs an evil shark to be destroyed or an evil Mafia against which a good capitalism can be defined. Rather, the sharks are everywhere and are all-pervading, as in the morality tale presented in Welles' *The Lady from Shanghai*. And like that tale, in Scorsese's films, these sharks inevitably end up devouring themselves.

We can see *Casino* as divided between the good middle-manager Rothstein and the evil excesses of Nicky Santoro. (Again, this is indicative of Scorsese's overall method: Bickle is contrasted with Sport (Harvey Keitel) in *Taxi Driver*, Amsterdam (Leonardo DiCaprio) and Bill the Butcher (Daniel Day Lewis) in *Gangs of New York*, the lawyer (Nick Nolte) and Max Cady (Robert DeNiro) in *Cape Fear*, Billy and Colin in *The Departed*). But Scorsese's point is this: even if one tries to be good and another is destined for evil, in the final account, the hero and the villain, good and evil, can barely be told apart because they are all enmeshed in an organization of misery. This is the final ethical commandment of Scorsese, which places him side by side with Kazan (whom he admires greatly): in America today, good can barely be found, and if it is there, it will only be quashed, snuffled, obliterated by the forces of evil. One only manages to fight evil by being more evil than evil itself so that at the end of *Casino*, Santoro is beaten to a pulp and buried alive alongside his brother who has been similarly beaten, or in *Gangs of New York* the only resolution is one in which the two gang leaders can both die at the hands of a police force which finally decides to unleash hell so that it is law and order itself that takes up the cause of evil, while in *The Departed*, body piles up upon body.

And yet, even amid all the carnage, somehow Scorsese manages to offer some kind of barely breathing 'life support' for the notion of a good America. The apocalyptic ending of *Gangs of New York* seems somehow resurrected by the final montage of the great New York rising from the ashes; in *The Departed* the evil Colin is finally murdered in one last act of redemptive violence from the man who seems to be the last remaining good cop; in *The Color of Money* Eddie, after years of being a cynical liquor importer – who has made a lot of money – is reborn ('I'm back', he shouts at the film's end), while in *Casino*, Rothstein is left to 'make do': he knows how to fiddle the numbers and play the right cards, so he merely finds a comfortable place in the hierarchy of the organization of misery. For Scorsese, the organization of misery is everywhere and one has to search long and hard to find one's way out of it. Scorsese thus inherits the Kazan of *Wild River*, but also the Griffith we have already seen in *A Corner in Wheat* or *Broken Blossoms*. If Scorsese shows us the greatness of the American dream and American cinema then he also shows us how this greatness has become the home of a decrepit, putrid, all-pervading misery.

Luc Besson: The *Cinéma du Look* or the Spectacle-Image

Luc Besson is representative of a kind of filmmaker that has emerged in the last thirty years or more (Ridley Scott and James Cameron are the two most prominent Hollywood representatives of this trend, though Quentin Tarantino, David Fincher and Christopher Nolan might also be found here) who combines a keen, dynamic visual sense adopted from advertising with a mode of storytelling indebted to television serials and 'Boys Own' adventure tales. The model for this approach is Lucas's *Star Wars* and if, as we have seen, one branch of dominant Hollywood grows from *Jaws* and Spielberg, then another branch grows from Lucas's blueprint for commercial success. There are three key aspects to this mode which we might call the spectacle-image: the triumph of spectacle; the fight or battle which is not sure quite what it is fighting for; and the invention of a blank form of pure evil from which the world must be rescued.

The Triumph of Spectacle. Deleuze discusses the senses of spectacle when writing of Fellini in *Cinema 2*. There he equates it with the ways in which Fellini fuses the spectacle with life, so that both are brought into question. The result is that spectacle functions there in its potential as a critique of life, as a critique of what might be defined as reality. If spectacle is important for Fellini (and no doubt it is for *Roma*, *Giulietta degli spiriti*, *8½* and many others) then it is important in so far as it offers a way out of reality, for it is a way of reinventing that reality – as indeed happens for Guido in *8½* or Giulietta in *Giulietta degli spiriti*. In the context of contemporary commercial cinema, however, spectacle functions in a rather different manner, a manner far more along the lines that Debord called the 'society of the spectacle' (Debord, 1994). That is, spectacle no longer carries with it the force of critique and reinvention that was possible with Fellini, but instead functions as an end in itself: the pure play of images, special effects, montages, sensations and sounds.

How does spectacle function, therefore, for a filmmaker like Besson? In *Subway* (1985), Besson borrows a number of images, plots and clichés from film history – from *Breathless*, from *Metropolis* (1927), *Fort Apache* (1948) and others – in order to . . . in order to what? Well, fundamentally, it is as though Besson wants to have fun with those images and clichés: he does not want to employ them in a mode of questioning or critique (as someone like the Godard of the 1960s does, for example), and nor does he employ them as worn out or as so many dead ends (as the 'new Hollywood' auteurs like Scorsese have done). Rather, the recycling of clichés is adopted by Besson as an end in itself. In this way, there is a certain kind of blankness to these plots and images so that we are unsure precisely what it is that Fred (Christopher Lambert) in *Subway* is fighting for or getting away from. He is not a figure of the underground resistance like the son in *Metropolis*, and nor is he the kind of misguided rebel we find in *Breathless* (though he comes close to this), nor is he a gangster of the type found in Hawks's *Scarface* (1932) (another of the film's reference points). And if Héléna (Isabelle Adjani) is akin to *Metropolis*'s Maria, then she is not there in order to save the world (as does Maria), but merely because she is bored with her older, bourgeois husband. For example, the scene of Héléna at the dinner party in which she abuses and admonishes her husband and his bourgeois friends – a fine scene indeed – fails as a critique of bourgeois mores in a manner that divorces it from Buñuel's great parody in *The Discreet Charm of the Bourgeoisie* (1972) (yet another of the film's references).

Besson's mode of spectacle is one of *pastiche* rather than critique or *parody*, to adopt once again a distinction drawn by Fredric Jameson: 'Pastiche is, like parody, the imitation of a peculiar or unique, idiosyncratic style [. . .]. But it is a neutral practice of such mimicry, without any of parody's ulterior motives, amputated of the satiric impulse' (Jameson, 1991, p. 17). We should not be critical of such blankness and spectacle, however, for Besson is merely presenting us with the blankness of contemporary existence, as was so deftly pointed out in Raphael Bassan's breakthrough essay on the *cinéma du look*:

> When you watch a film by Antonioni, you know that it will end badly [. . .]. But with [Jean-Jaqcues] Beineix, Besson and [Leos] Carax, you get a combination of playfulness and the death or the failure of the 'heroes'. All the seductive elements (neon lights, extravagant hairstyles, hi-tech hi fi, and so on) are negatively connoted. They are no longer signs of being, but signs of death (Bassan, 2007, p. 18).

The Struggle Against What or Whom? The consequences of spectacle and its mode of pastiche is that Besson's plots tend to deliver a hero who needs to fight against something which we know is supposed to be bad or evil, but we are never quite certain what it is that makes this enemy bad or evil. One might easily interpret such a move as akin to the ways in which the American Indians of classic Westerns are treated – in *Stagecoach*, for example, it is taken as read that the Indians are bad and that they may – and most probably will – attack (which they eventually do, of course), or, for much the same reasons, such plots might be harking back to the kinds of Negroes we see in *Birth of a Nation*, or even as reminiscent of the evil aliens one finds in classic science fiction films like *The Thing from Another World* (1951), *The Day the Earth Stood Still* (1951) or *Invasion of the Body Snatchers* (1956). But Besson gives us something rather different from these, for in those films from classical Hollywood, there was always a civilization at stake so that the struggles for supremacy over an ill-defined 'evil' were nonetheless struggles for the founding of a nation, a society, a civilization.

For Besson's plots, on the contrary, there seems to be very little at stake. Phil Powrie will therefore remark that, if the characters of Besson's films appear alienated, 'it is at least partly, if the films are to be believed, because there is no depth in the postmodern (including the socio-political postmodern of all promise of great reforms and no substance), only surface, and therefore nothing to believe in anymore' (Powrie, 2007, p. 75). Such claims reiterate some earlier arguments on *Subway* in which Powrie discovered a pleasurable masochism in Fred, the film's hero, in as much as this character suffers from a kind of resignation in which nothing much seems to matter anymore. This masochism is pleasurable, Powrie goes on to argue, 'because it is predicated on the abdication of responsibility: an anomic retreat from the difficult and necessary negotiation of community' (Powrie, 1997, p. 129). If this is a hero of the contemporary world, then it is a very different sort of hero from that of the classical movement-image. We find something very similar in *The Big Blue* (1988), a hero who is helpless and who has only known a world that continually abandons him (his father, his mother, his best friend). And much the same goes for *Leon* (1994) – a hit man with no past or future; a young girl divorced from family and home – as well as *Joan of Arc* (1999).

This process, however, is most evident in *Nikita* (1990). Here, Nikita (Anne Parillaud), a young rebel-punk – a proto-terrorist of the masochistic type akin to the one we find in *Subway* – is captured by the police and retrained so that she can become a special police operative. Once trained, she effectively becomes a machine for carrying out orders – perhaps akin to the kinds of subjects of the 'state apparatus' Deleuze and Guattari analyse in *A Thousand Plateaus* (Deleuze and Guattari, 1987, p. 375) – so that neither she nor we as viewers of the film get to know *why* or for *what reason* she kills the people whom she is ordered to kill. Rather, we merely know that she is presented with orders and that she must carry out those orders without any rhyme or reason. We are given *some* insight into Nikita's final assignment – to stop a foreign diplomat from smuggling plans out of the country – but we are never given information as to the specific nature of these plans and their possible threat to national security (or whatever the threat might be). Even her attempts to settle down and engage in a romance seem like so many pre-scripted lines of a hip, young, upwardly-mobile life that has been pre-planned. If she does manage to escape at the end of the film, then perhaps this is a vision of the only way to survive in this world: to flee, escape (or find a 'line of flight', as Deleuze and Guattari will advise).

What is evident here is what Deleuze refers to as a 'control society'. If the modern world – from the end of the eighteenth century through to the late twentieth century – offers a *disciplinary society* of the kind described by Michel Foucault in *Discipline and Punish*, then more recently there has emerged what Foucault and Deleuze call a *society of control*. What is specific to the first of these, societies of discipline, is that they are established on the basis of an ethics of good and evil so that human subjects will be 'subjectivized' in accordance with the principles of the good. We have seen as much at play in the classic films and auteurs of the movement-image. In control societies, by contrast, there is no longer a choice between good and evil, for the good is decided in advance for us by officials or by police forces more powerful than we (and today, more often than not, the good is aligned with money). All we can do in such a society is to operate in accordance with the laws prescribed for us, in accordance with the codes, instructions, information and strictures that are pre-planned for us. And this is what happens to Nikita: if for the first half of the film she is imprisoned in a manner that accords with a disciplinary society – where she is rehabilitated and learns how to become a 'proper subject' – then for the second half of the film, when she is set 'free', as it were, she accepts her freedom only on the basis of being controlled by the police force for which she has been trained. She does not fight or kill in the name of the good over a force depicted as evil, she merely does what she is ordered to do.

The Invention of a Blank Form of Pure Evil from which the World must be Rescued. In Besson's films, these characters, for the most part, still find the time to fight against something, but the contours of that something are more than a little hazy. If there are still enemies to be defeated, how are these enemies defined? How does this enemy function? For *The Fifth Element* (1997), a film clearly indebted to Roland Emmerich's *Independence Day* (1996), even in all of its emptiness, the enemy is made explicit: it is nothing less than absolute evil, an enormous ball of death and destruction that threatens to destroy all life. There is no reason behind this absolute evil: it does not want to destroy life for any particular end, but rather is bent on destruction purely because that is what it does. Blended with this is a mystico–religious subplot about the secret power of the 'fifth element' needed to ensure that the forces of good prevail over those of absolute evil (adapted, one suspects, from Spielberg's *Indiana Jones* films). And *The Fifth Element* is symptomatic of a whole politico–social order of the present and to hosts of films made over the last thirty years or more – beginning with *Star Wars*, but working through the *Alien* (1979, 1986, 1992, 1997) and *Terminator* films (1984, 1991, 2003, 2009), reaching watershed moments in *Independence Day* and *The Matrix* (1999) and many others, up to Christopher Nolan's recent *Inception* (2010). Jacques Rancière has realized the significance of these scenarios for the cinema:

> Before the aliens, it was the landing of the Reds in Los Angeles or San Francisco that we awaited. In those times, the sureness of American victory was that of the victory of freedom and democracy over their mortal enemies. One fought, or one feigned to fight, to find out whether it was better to be 'red' or 'dead'. Since we no longer risk being red, the threat of death is all that remains, so the slogan of the supreme combat can be stated simply: better alive than dead (Rancière, 2010a, p. 17).

The demise of communism has left the western democracies without an enemy; or at the very least, without an enemy that poses an alternative socio–political framework (the absolute evil of Islam, of Saddam Hussein's Iraq or Al Quaida are of an entirely different order from the 'old' communism). Rather, now the only alternative posited against the western democracies is that of an indefinable absolute evil – death itself, as a film like *The Fifth Element* makes so clear. But it is there too in *Nikita*, for Nikita goes on with her life even if this means giving up all of her individual freedoms (her comrades are all killed at the film's opening), while Fred in *Subway*, Jacques (Jean-Marc Barr) in *The Big Blue* and Leon choose death rather than face the intolerability of a control society. The message here is that *there is no alternative*: choose a life that is intolerable, for the only alternative choice is envisaged as absolute evil. Is it any wonder that Nikita, Fred, Jacques and Leon make the choices they do, or that Joan of Arc's fate still resonates with our own? And as for *The Fifth Element*, even this film seems to acknowledge the futility or stupidity of its own fight against 'absolute evil', as though the whole film really is some kind of joke (even if one must admit that it is not an especially funny one). It is as though with Besson's films and some of the others I have mentioned, the movement-image can barely believe in itself any more.

Deleuze was astute enough to see this coming when he compared control societies with those of the disciplinary age: 'Compared with the approaching forms of ceaseless control in open sites, we may come to see the harshest confinement as part of a wonderful happy past' (Deleuze, 1995, p. 175). There is perhaps no need for me to declare that I look back on the film worlds of Griffith, Eisenstein, Hawks, Hitchcock and others as part of a wonderful happy cinematic past.

10

Cinema After Deleuze (II): Recent Elements of the Time-Image

Lars von Trier: A Cinema Against Ethics

In Lars von Trier's *The Idiots* (1998), a group a pseudo-radical experimentalists play-act at being 'idiots' – at being mentally retarded. At one point during the film, their play-acting leads them to engage in a game of group sex, a 'gang bang'. This leads us to question the motivations of the group's leader, Stoffer (Jens Albinus), for he is the one who suggests the gang bang. Does he want the members of the group to experience a sense of uninhibited sexual play in which bourgeois codes of monogamous propriety are undone? That is, does he want them to pursue sex for its own sake, as radically separated from the sentimental attachments of love or possession? Or, quite to the contrary, does Stoffer just want to 'fuck his friends' (Smith, 2003, p. 115)? Such a dilemma pushes us to the central question not only of *The Idiots* but of the entirety of von Trier's work: does he ask his characters to do morally reprehensible things in order to fulfil the radical aspiration of offending and upsetting ingrained sensibilities; or does he have his characters do morally reprehensible things in order to fulfil his own perverse desires, in order that he 'get his kicks'?

There are no clear answers to such questions – and indeed if there seems to be any guiding thread to von Trier's techniques and projects, then more than anything that seems to be one of 'trying things out' to see what happens, to never rest on his laurels, to always try *new* things. (He states that his guiding idea for *The Idiots* was that 'I had the idea of a group of people who chose to act like idiots – no more than that' (von Trier, 2003a, p. 204).) His characters do morally reprehensible things so as to offend moral decencies, but this does not therefore mean that these characters then successfully undermine such moral decencies or provide alternatives to the status quo. Rather, the alternatives offered by such characters are usually as problematic as those to which they are opposed. If Stoffer quite rightly points out that bourgeois standards need to be undermined, then he can also only do so in as much as he is offered a sanctuary in which to do so by a rich uncle (the members of the group in *The Idiots* live temporarily at the uncle's house) thus demonstrating that the undermining of the bourgeoisie must itself be propped up by the bourgeoisie (in much the same way as occurs in Godard's *La Chinoise*). To further this point, the group also indulges in a party by virtue of the gold credit card of one of the group's members, Axel, an advertising executive fully enmeshed in bourgeois self-hatred. And even if the intentions of the group appear noble – that is, to demonstrate the virtues of outsiders; to show us that idiots might be the inhabitants of a higher humanity – then at times they also appear irreparably cruel, as occurs when genuinely retarded people visit, or when it becomes clear that one of the group's participants, Josephine, is mentally unstable, or in the film's closing sequence in which Karen, having recently lost her daughter, play-acts in front of her sister's family. Here, at these moments, 'spassing' (as the group calls it) appears entirely inappropriate.

Such inadequacies leave von Trier's films open. In simple terms, if films of the movement-image, as Deleuze designates them, allow us to clearly discern the difference between good and evil, then von Trier's films make impossible such discernment. Von Trier offers us images freed from judgement. Von Trier does not pass judgement and if the spectators of these films do judge them then such judgements are the result of those spectators' own sensibilities more than they are products of the films themselves. (Murray Smith, for example, eagerly wants to criticize the immorality of the 'spassers' in *The Idiots* or the naivety of von Trier's provocations in *The Five Obstructions* (2003) (see Smith, 2008), as though the higher moral ground of these films is the one in which they can be shown to have failed.) If we find Jan's or Bess's behaviour repugnant in *Breaking the Waves* (1996), then that is because *we* judge them, for the film itself refuses to pass its judgement on them. Certainly, there are characters which some of the films will judge – Fisher (Michael Elphick) in *The Element of Crime* (1984), those of the strict religious sect in *Breaking the Waves*, the legal system itself in *Dancer in the Dark* (2000) – but this is precisely the point: the films will judge those who themselves pass judgement or who seek to judge. Like Vargas in Welles's *Touch of Evil*, the characters in von Trier's films who avidly seek justice often end up being the most morally questionable: Stoffer in *The Idiots*, Fisher in *The Element of Crime*, Tom and Grace in *Dogville* (2003), Grace in *Manderlay* (2005). For von Trier, the man or woman who cries 'truth' is contrasted with the faker, the imposter, the outsider: Leopold in *Europa* (1991), Osbourne in *The Element of Crime*, Willem in *Manderlay*, Selma in *Dancer in the Dark*. 'The truthful man', writes Deleuze, 'in the end wants nothing other than to judge life; he holds up a superior value, the good, in the name of which he will be able to judge, he is craving to judge, he sees in life an evil, a fault which is to be atoned: the moral origin of the notion of truth' (Deleuze, 1989, p. 137). Such is the man (or woman) of truth whom von Trier aims to criticize. Against the supreme moralist of truth is posited the human being with the capacity, as Deleuze puts it, 'for evaluating every being, every action and passion, even every value in relation to the life which they involve' (ibid., p. 141). And here we can recognize the purest of von Trier's heroines, Selma: '*She is someone who loves all of life.* She can feel intensely about the miracles that every corner of her (fairly grim) life offers. And she can see all the details . . . every single one' (von Trier, 2003a, p. 237).

Breaking the Waves shows some of the difficulties of von Trier's approach to the question of judgement. The film appears critical of the institutions of religion along with the medical and legal professions. And yet, Bess's own religiosity sits somewhere between the ridiculous and the sublime, at once astonishingly naïve and deluded, but at the same time with reparative effects and a saintly glow: at all times Bess is seen as the one member of the community who possesses a 'true' faith, a faith that is not archaically rule bound and overtly repressive. There is something here of the attempt to establish a 'belief in this world', as Deleuze would put it, and von Trier's admiration for Dreyer in this respect is well documented. But the doctor, Richardson, the voice of reason in the film, presents the most curious dilemma, for he is, on the one hand, full of admiration for Bess and her 'goodness', while on the other hand, he is also cruel or jealous enough to demand her separation from Jan, the great love of her life. To this end, he invokes his medical expertise (tinged with its legal requirements) in order to consign Bess to medical care. Dr Richardson, a character of sympathy and goodness, is also capable of demeaning cruelty.

If we accept this as a position that von Trier's films typically take – that which emphasizes the indiscernibility of good and evil – then Jacques Rancière goes so far as to claim that his works are representative of an end to the fight for justice over injustice (Rancière, 2010b). All that is left now is a world in which evil and injustice have triumphed and there is no vision of good or justice that might restore greatness or rightness to this world. *Dogville* is perhaps most emphatic here, for the endearingly good character, Grace, can only end the film by siding with the forces of the greater evil (the gangsters) against the lesser evil (the townspeople of Dogville). The only solution to injustice is a greater injustice. Or, as Rancière goes on to argue, the only justice is that which is invoked to protect the community, not in the name of the good or a better world, but rather in the name of merely protecting those whose stakes might be under threat. Thus, the small town community of Dogville cannot ultimately accept its outsider (Grace) and nor can the gangster father accept that which might damage his own interests. The only way of dealing with the outsider is to punish, expel or exterminate him or her. If we compare *Dogville* with Kazan's *Wild River*, for example, then the outsider (Chuck Glover) in Kazan's film is finally accepted by the small town and family as a representative of a potentially better world, even in spite of the initial hostility towards him. By contrast, if Grace is initially accepted in the town of Dogville, then after a while the townspeople decide they cannot accept her seemingly strange acts and beliefs. Rather, anything which cannot be understood is ultimately condemned. From this perspective, von Trier charts the stakes of the contemporary impossibility of encountering the outside.

Matters become still more complicated in *Manderlay*. There, all attempts at founding the good or a good society of equals leads to catastrophe. Ultimately, the Negro slaves of this film settle for 'the lesser of two evils', for the slavery which they had known turns out to be more compatible with a potential happiness than the purported freedom that Grace bestows upon them. In that prior structure of slavery, the community of Negroes knew who and what they were supposed to hate – their 'Mam', the plantation owner – so that their community could be safely structured as a unified whole bounded by an outside ('evil') which could be negated. Such an enclosed community is what Rancière refers to as an 'ethical' community, a community from which opposition and political antagonism have been eradicated. We might argue therefore that von Trier's vision of the contemporary world is one which shows us the ethical consensus of today's neoliberal capitalist societies.

If von Trier's films demonstrate the difficulty of judgement – if they show us that injustice is all too prevalent in a manner which makes it virtually impossible to judge what is good and what is evil – then this is part of a demand to truly expose to us 'the unthought in thought'. Von Trier dares to show us what we might not ourselves dare to think; he shows us that which today has been excluded from thought. From this perspective Rancière is indeed correct when he writes that today:

> there is no status for the excluded in the structuration of the community. On the one hand, the excluded is merely the one who accidentally falls outside the great equality of all – the sick, the retarded or the forsaken to whom the community must extend a hand in order to re-establish the social bond. On the other, the excluded becomes the radical other, the one who is separated from the community for the mere fact of being alien to it, of not sharing the identity that binds each to all, and of threatening the community in each of us (Rancière, 2010b, p. 116).

We can notice here a cast of von Trier's outsiders: Bess in *Breaking the Waves*, Grace in *Dogville*, Selma in *Dancer in the Dark*, the 'spassers' in *The Idiots*. But more than anything we can also notice a strategy of von Trier, that of injecting into a film precisely what offends thought, what offends anything deemed right and proper to the ongoing structuration of a community. 'What's important to me with a film', von Trier has declared, 'is that you use an impeccable technique to tell people a story that they don't want to be told' (von Trier, 2003b, p. 10). And this is precisely what is at stake for von Trier's offensive gestures: to show us what we barely dare to think, the unthought in thought, that form of thinking which comes from the 'outside', a story we don't want to be told.

To put things another way, from Deleuze's perspective we might say that von Trier tries to introduce a little psychosis into a world structured by neurosis (Deleuze's most succinct expression of this argument occurs in his small essay on Herman Melville's novella 'Bartleby the Scrivener'; see Deleuze, 1998b). Let us consider *Breaking the Waves* as a distant remake of Kazan's *Splendor in the Grass* (1961). Kazan's film charts the great American-Freudian neurosis, that of sexual repression, of teenagers desperately in love but unable to consummate that love because it contravenes social and religious codes. Warren Beatty delivers a rousing performance as the young buck whose desire must be held in check and whose life, thoughts, body and outlook become contorted and broken by this repression. By contrast, Bess in *Breaking the Waves* sidesteps her religious elders by marrying Jan, and their honeymoon period of sexual ecstasy is one born of the lifting of neurotic repressions and paternal mandates, a kind of sexual madness that directly shatters the Puritanism of the deeply religious community. And it is in this distinction that we can discover the originality of von Trier's methods: if films of the movement-image try to compose communities that are bounded by laws and moral frameworks which will allow the establishment of a way of being or even of a new order of things – the birth of a nation, no less – then films of the time-image, such as those of von Trier, are dedicated to questioning and undermining all the ways in which communities have been established in the modern world. If an alternative is suggested (the sexual deliverance of Bess and Jan; the community of 'idiots' or 'slaves') then these communities do not necessarily provide viable alternatives. Rather, what von Trier proposes is a decomposition of accepted views, a continued questioning of the unquestioned foundational views by which we commonly live and by means of which we are encouraged to live in common. Stories we do not want to be told and characters who do improper things: this is the key to von Trier's method.

Wong Kar-Wai: The Floating-Image

The films of Wong Kar-wai are perhaps unique in so far as they seem to begin and end *in medias res*. Even in films like *Ashes of Time* (1994) or *As Tears Go By* (1988), films that have more or less traditional story arcs, we still begin in the middle of startling action scenes and end at something only vaguely resembling an 'ending' (*As Tears Go By* might be the only of Wong's films to properly feature an ending). The reason for this is that Wong works with memory images and his entire oeuvre might be a response to the hero's proclamation near the end of *Ashes of Time*: 'The more you try to forget something, the more it'll stick in your memory'. Memory is never finished with, it keeps reappearing, it keeps coming back, it keeps reinventing itself. Wong's films are thus compositions of 'pure recollection' in Bergson's sense. They chart the various journeys of their characters in terms of their insertions into sheets of past, their attempts to plunge into and relive the past. And this is never a past that reaches any sort of moment of conclusion as though there is a definitive lesson to be learned from the mistakes or victories of the past. Here, there is no Terry Malloy who realizes he took a wrong turn in his past so that he can now resolve to correct that past and follow a right and true course. Instead, in Wong's films there is a continual working over of the past, an attempt to work out the past, to replay, resurrect and remember again. These characters confront their pasts almost as though they might be the pasts of someone other than themselves while the frequent use of voiceover narration adds a subjective commentary to images which the characters try to approach as in some way objective.

In a fine scene in *Happy Together* (1997), a film which is a recollection in its entirety, there are also moments when the narrative comes to a halt and the lead character Fai suddenly interjects with a reminiscence. When Fai's lover, Po-Wing, is injured, Fai nurses him back to health. When Fai realizes Po-Wing has gotten better and that he no longer needs Fai to look after him, there emerges a startled recollection. It is separated from the rest of the surrounding images by its grainy black and white features (as used elsewhere in the film) and Fai's voiceover. He realizes that he hadn't wanted Po-Wing to recover quite so quickly, that the days of his convalescence were their happiest, that he didn't want them to end. It is in scenes like these that we get Wong's indications of how memory works: is this flash of black and white a *virtual subjective* recollection that captures the intimate affective remembrance of Fai's love for Po-Wing? And in contrast to this moment, are the surrounding coloured images *actual objective* ones which chart the progress and disintegration of the romance in an 'objective' way? The answer to such questions is *neither*. In fact, the black and white moment of voiceover narration might even be said to be more objective than the other images, in so far as Fai is able to reflect upon them, to now realize that, above and beyond their insertion into a romantic tale of their love, these images are the most objective distillation of the intensity and passion of their being 'happy together'. Here then, Wong delivers to us the clearest expression of a time-image: that in which actual and virtual, past and present, become indiscernible.

This scene of black and white flashback is then followed shortly after by another extraordinary moment, a bizarre exchange of scenes in which past and present become definitively blurred: a workmate (with whom Fai will soon become close friends) asks Fai out for a drink; Fai throws up; and these actions are all interspersed with images of Po-Wing's departure, with the concluding sense that this time Po-Wing has left for good: their relationship is over. These images occur in a shotgun manner, too quick to notice, too muddled to immediately understand, but they effectively communicate the shock and anguish of Fai's realization that Po-Wing really has gone this time, and he will not be back. It is a breaking up in which the images and memories themselves 'break up' as though Fai cannot quite manage an order of the virtual that could possibly pass over into the actual, a presence of the past that is still too intense to be effectively experienced as present or definitively consigned to the past. Here again Wong shows us exemplary time-images.

Almost at the end of *Cinema 1*, when writing of the 'crisis of the action-image', Deleuze mentions in passing a notion of 'floating images':

> They are these floating images, these anonymous clichés, which circulate in the external world, but which also penetrate each one of us and constitute his internal world, so that everyone possesses only psychic clichés by which he thinks and feels, is thought and is felt, being himself a cliché among the others in the world which surrounds him (Deleuze, 1986, pp. 208–9).

Wong's films take up the challenge of the clichéd world in ways that neither Scorsese nor Besson do (from our discussions in Chapter 9). If cliché in Scorsese merely emphasizes a world of misery and if in Besson the cliché merely re-emphasizes and universalizes its operations, then for Wong the cliché emerges only in order that it is negated and broken (for such a ploy, see Deleuze, 1989, p. 20). Clichés are everywhere in Wong: the warrior or swordplay heritage (*Wuxia pian*) of *Ashes of Time*, the gangster genre in *As Tears Go By*, the cop drama in *Chunking Express* (1994), the romantic stereotypes of *In the Mood for Love* (2000), the road or travel movie in *Happy Together*. There are also the clichés of a universalized Americanized commodity existence: from fast food (especially the tinned varieties) to pop songs ('California Dreamin', 'Happy Together', 'Take my Breath Away'), the pulp novels of *In the Mood* to the tango and cigarettes in *Happy Together*.

All of these clichéd contents are backed up by the formal qualities of the images: if the clichés themselves are floating objects, gestures and mannerisms which float independently of their subjective intentions – the characters are enveloped by or perform by virtue of these clichéd surroundings – then it is the manipulation of images themselves, the ways they look and sound, that are also made to float. Ackbar Abbas's analyses have been crucial in this respect. Of the martial arts scenes in *Ashes of Time* he writes that:

> It is no longer a choreography of human bodies in motion that we see. In fact, we do not know what it is that we are seeing. Things have now been speeded up to such an extent that what we

find is only a composition of light and colour – a kind of abstract expressionism or action painting (Abbas, 1997, p. 32).

And of the many techniques Wong uses to emphasize slow motion or of his many uses of staggered, stop motion blurring, Abbas writes that

> Slow motion [. . .] is not being used [. . .] to romanticize or aestheticize either love or violence; it is used analytically to study, to understand. But analysis by slow motion, like analysis by blowup, leads at a certain point only to a blurring of the image, that is, to bewilderment rather than understanding. The closer you look, the less there is to see (ibid., p. 35).

These 'floating-images' are ungrounded, they straggle, wander, as though set free on a breeze or at other times as though thrown into some sort of sound and image blender. Wong's constant and unique manipulations of colour and grain only add to this floatingness. And finally, the obsession with memory delivers, in combination with the other ingredients, a sense of a flow of images that never comes to rest, never reaches an end point, but rather circulates round and round, never settling anywhere. As the characters keep on emphasizing in *Happy Together*, 'Let's start over'.

Abbas tries to describe this overall sense in terms of what he calls the *déjà disparu*. This notion is indebted to Deleuze's constructions in *Cinema 2*, for it characterizes the sense in which the present is always passing, that time is split between past and present, that one can never put one's finger on the present because it is always passing away; that the present only emerges as a fading memory because it is always disappearing right before our eyes, slipping from our grasp. But this only gives us part of the story, for what is even more important in Wong's films is his revisiting of the senses of time evoked by Resnais: *sheets of past* and *peaks of present*. Wong's characters are always trying to reinsert themselves into the past – into sheets of past – while at the same time trying to emphasize or relive the very presentness of those moments of the past – they try to access these moments as *peaks of present*. We find such strategies prominent in *Ashes of Time* and *Happy Together*, but it is in the masterpiece *In the Mood for Love* that Wong takes this approach to its highest point. The great effect of *In the Mood for Love* occurs as a process of realizing that we are merely watching the lead character's recollections of a lost love, of something which was close to love, or perhaps something closer, more intense and more evocative than the kinds of loves characterized by marriages and long term futures. Romantic, certainly, in the sense that a first person novel can be (a Proustian sensibility haunts this film, especially in the details, a brushing of clothes, the colour of a tie, the taste of a meal, the books on a shelf). These memory-images seem to float, as though they are freed from the Earth's gravity. The images are of a dream-like variety, a combination of the acute angles, the camera's finding its way through partially blocked windows and doorways, the saturated colours, the slow-motion effects and the nostalgic soundtrack.

Dominating the film is the sense of trying to recapture the moments, the feelings and sensations – the 'mood' – of this romance. We are very close to Resnais's *Last Year at Marienbad* here, especially of X's attempts to convince A that they met last year, that last year they were very much in the mood for love. So too with *In the Mood for Love* there are several sheets of past that the hero turns over and travels through, but intertwined with these sheets are the peaks of present: the specific moments, the attempts within those pure recollections of past to make those pasts present again. Hence the intensity of those fleeting but magical moments of connectedness between the couple. And, of course, the key scenes of 'play-acting' in which the heroine imagines breaking up with her husband: 'This is just a rehearsal', she states; 'This isn't real' she adds at another point. And we know that in his memory the man is regretting that this wasn't just a rehearsal, all the while knowing all too well that these experiences were real, indeed that their play-acting was real. And now, after this time, as he looks back, he realizes that these memories are definitively real, even as they are virtual. They are all that is left of that time. And, as an objective statement of the man's subjective state (that is, as a blurring of the objective and the subjective), at the end of the film the intertitles declare: 'That era has passed; nothing that belonged to it exists any more'. Wong delivers exemplary time-images

Abbas Kiarostami: The Open Image

Influenced by Deleuze, Shohini Chaudhuri and Howard Finn propose a characterization of recent Iranian cinema in terms of what they call the 'open image' (Chaudhuri and Finn, 2003). Abbas Kiarostami is perhaps the most internationally noted of these filmmakers (though Mohsen Makhmalbaf is certainly as significant, if not more so), and his films offer what are exemplary 'open images'. Chaudhuri and Finn argue that their notion of an open image is very similar to what Deleuze designates as the crystal-image. The crystalline or open structure (we shall get to the finer distinctions later) arises via an aesthetic indebted to Italian neorealism combined with a prominently foregrounded reflexivity. Kiarostami's films (and those of many other recent Iranian directors) adopt something akin to the naïve camera of neorealism – the use of shots of long duration and of shooting in depth, as well as the use of 'journey' structures and plots – but this is often combined with an intense reflexivity: many of these films are as much about filmmaking and films within films as they are about anything else. Makhmalbaf's *Salaam Cinema* (1995) and *A Moment of Innocence* (1996) were groundbreaking in this respect, but following *Where is the Friend's House?* (1987), all of Kiarostami's films adopt a foregrounded reflexivity of some sort. *Where is the Friend's House?*, for example, eventually becomes entwined in a series of films – *Life and Nothing More . . .* (1992), *The Wind Will Carry Us* (1999), *Through the Olive Trees* (1994) – that all gesture back to *Where is the Friend's House?* in quite overt ways.

This will constitute the first level of the crystal: that of the melding of a film with the lives from which those films have blossomed. *Where is the Friend's House?* centres on the genesis of the friendship between two school friends, Ahmed and Mohamed, in the remote rural town of Koker. These characters are played by 'natural actors', that is, Ahmed and Mohamed really were schoolboys from the region, so that in pursuing such strategies, Kiarostami is clearly demonstrating his indebtedness to the child films of the neorealists (*Bicycle Thieves, Germany, Year Zero* [1948]). But when a year later there was a devastating earthquake in the region, Kiarostami decided to go back in order to find out what might have happened to the two boys, so that *Life and Nothing More . . .* finds itself positioned somewhere between a documentary and fiction as we search in 'real life' for the fictional characters from Kiarostami's earlier film. Ahmed and Mohamed then reappear – shall we call them 'cameos'? – in *Through the Olive Trees*, which again builds much of its plot around the real events of the earthquake that had occurred a few short years earlier. And here the film within a film is foregrounded, for *Through the Olive Trees* is as much about the filming of a stunted romance between Hossein and Tahereh as it is about the charting a 'real' romance between the couple. All the while, of course, this film and its film within a film are framed by the intrusion of the real devastation of the earthquake, so that when Hossein is supposed to say, according to the script of the film within the film, that he lost 65 members of his extended family, he retorts with the 'fact' that 'no, it was really only 25'. This is the first level of the crystal: the intertwined layers of the 'filmic' and the 'real'.

This first state of the crystal will emerge in different ways in other films. In *Close-Up* (1990) we have a film purportedly based on the true story of a man who is a great admirer of Makhmalbaf's films, who tries to then pass himself off as the director himself. And he does so successfully for a short period of time, only to eventually be caught by the police and put on trial. The trial footage is shot with grainy video (or is it 16mm blown up to 35mm?)[1] so that it is supposed to evoke more 'realness' than the other recreations. At the trial the imposter will try to argue that he felt more true, more like himself, or at the very least that he felt like *somebody* while he was acting as Makhmalbaf; it delivered to him a sense of true subjectivity that his everyday self could not. The crystalline features are thus emerging: where does real life end and impersonation begin? Additionally, we have a fake film based on a true story in which a real filmmaker is involved. Finally, at the end of the film, the imposter meets the real Makhmalbaf, while secretly being filmed by the film crew (the film crew that is supposed to be making *this* film so that we once again have a kind of documentary within the film) who, in turn, have sound problems when filming this scene, foregrounding for us the processes of what it is or can be to make a film. Kiarostami constructs crystals of dazzling complexity.

10 (2002) provides a different kind of crystal-image. In so many ways reminiscent of Ophüls's *La ronde* we are shown a series of ten interactions that the main character, Shiva, encounters while driving around Tehran in her car. There is no overt chronology here, so that we are uncertain as to precisely what the relations between the episodes are. When Shiva's son Amin jumps in the passenger seat for the fourth time at the end of the film, there is no indication as to what period of time might have passed since he was last in that seat, nor of what events might have transpired during that time. But most prominent is the film's technique: shot in digital video, entirely from small video cameras mounted on the car's dashboard, with one camera pointed at the driver's seat, and the other pointed at the passenger's seat. The documentary-style starkness of the images jars our senses in the ways that, say, Rouch's *Chronicle of a Summer* (1961) or, more recently, *The Blair Witch Project* (1999) might have done. Kiarostami's use of digital video seems a long way away from von Trier's, for the staginess and audacity of von Trier's approach is vastly different from the naïve directness of Kiarostami's camera eye so that the juxtaposition of (fictional) story and (documentary) fact pushes and resonates across the film. Kiarostami will utilize this digital video starkness once again with *Shirin* (2008), a film of people watching a film, so that, at one and the same time, we try to follow via sonic cues the film this audience is watching but which we cannot see, while at the same time the film we are watching is that of the responses and reactions of these audience members. Added to this, the film that the audience within the film watches is an ancient Persian tale of female love and oppression (or oppression via love), a theme also confronted in *10* and most recently in *Certified Copy* (2010). The audience members, all of whom are female (there are one or two men who occasionally appear obscured in the background), then register this oppression in their expressions and affects which respond to the film within a film that they watch. These are therefore the layers upon layers of crystalline constructions which Kiarostami builds into his films.

Chaudhuri and Finn concentrate on another aspect – call this the second aspect of the crystal in Kiarostami: the endings of the films. *Through the Olive Trees* concludes, for example, with an entirely ambiguous long shot – long both in terms of duration and distance – as Hossein follows Tahereh through the olive trees and across a field, far into the distance, only to then return and retrace his steps back through the field and olive trees. Has he succeeded in winning Tahereh's love? One suspects not, but in a sense that Kiarostami very much intends, the film is here 'set free': 'The film-maker has carried the film up to here, and now it is given up to the audience to think about it and watch these characters from very far away' (Kiarostami quoted in Chaudhuri and Finn, 2003, p. 49). It is as though this 'bit' of the film is disconnected from the rest of the film so that it reflects back on the rest of the film, throws it into relief and places it into a new light. This process of the film's turning back on itself gives to us another state of the crystal-image. *The Taste of Cherry* (1997) delivers a reflexive ending with full force: for most of the film, the hero Badii is trying to find someone to help him to commit suicide. His plan is to lie down in a hole he has dug on a hillside on the outskirts of Tehran and take a whole packet of sleeping pills. He assumes this will kill him, but he needs someone to come by the hole the following morning so as to properly bury him, to cover him with twenty spadefuls of dirt. He asks several people and after many refusals, he finally gets the agreement of one wise man who espouses to him the joys of the fullness of life, the wonder of the taste of cherries and the beauty of watching a sunrise and so on. Night falls, our hero lies down in the hole he has dug and the screen fades to black. When the sunshine returns (the following morning?) there are only grainy video shots of a film crew – the film crew of *this* film, no less, with Kiarostami himself, not to mention the actor playing Badii (Homayoun Ershadi) who wanders from here to there smoking a cigarette. And Kiarostami even declares here that 'The shoot is finished', that 'we are only here for a sound take' (the sound we hear is of soldiers marching, a sound which has been played two or three times during the film). Here again, therefore, we have an ending of the film which throws the entire rest of the film into some sort of relief, which resets the dimensions and expectations we had been building throughout the entire film. But will he kill himself? Will the other man come and bury him? Did he take the sleeping pills? All of these questions which seemed to us to be guiding the film are quashed and undone; they are not questions that will be answered, for 'the shoot is done'. And we have already mentioned the ending of *Close-Up*: the imposter is rewarded by meeting his hero, Makhmalbaf, so that all his impositions and fakery are retrieved triumphantly.

Chaudhuri and Finn argue that these endings allow the films to 'live on' after the film itself has finished. Of *The Taste of Cherry* they argue that 'The switch from night and death to day and life, far from resolving the narrative, creates an ambiguity, an openness, as if we are now watching images of life after death' (Chaudhuri and Finn, 2003, p. 52). It is this openness or ambiguity of the image that Chaudhuri and Finn call the 'open image', a crystal-image which foregrounds its ambiguity and lack of resolution, but the endings of which also open out the remainder of the film, reopen its pasts in the light of the open and unresolved presents of the endings. They add that 'The best open images "open up" the films in which they appear (turn the films into crystal images) and open films "out" to the world' (ibid., p. 56). Kiarostami, the key example for these authors, certainly provides brilliant crystalline, open images.

Might there be more at stake, however, for Kiarostami? Might he offer, more than anything else, a belief in this world? The endings of the films are like gifts from the gods which descend into this world: the wonderful ending of *Where is My Friend's House?* in which, even though he does not find the friend's house, and even if he cannot return his workbook to him, nevertheless, the next day, his friend's homework is done (for he has done the friend's homework for him) and he will not be punished by the teacher. It is a wonderful, miraculous act of friendship in so far as he discovers that such acts are possible and that such acts can make this world something to believe in, outside of the rules and regulations of the classroom or the boy's parents (and not to mention all the wonderful sights and meetings the boy has encountered during his search for the friend's house). All these discoveries are so many ways of restoring belief in the world. In *The Taste of Cherry* the stakes of belief are more upfront, especially in the wise man's story of how he had once tried to kill himself by hanging himself from a mulberry tree, but when he tasted the mulberries and saw the setting sun from high up in the tree, he decided not to go through with it. 'A mulberry saved my life' he says. And he advises the film's hero to think carefully before taking his own life, for 'The world isn't the way you see it'; 'You have to change your outlook to change the world' . . . 'You want to give up the taste of cherries?'. This man's declarations are nothing less than assertions of his restored belief in this world (he works at the nearby Natural History Museum). And it does not matter whether the film's hero eventually does kill himself or not, for when we are awoken from the dark of night into the brightness of video daylight it is as if we have been reawakened into this world, that the film itself flashed us out of our stupor and into a clarified reality.

Even a film as seemingly as abstract as *Shirin* can achieve this too: the full force and relevance of an ancient Persian tale receives its full resonance when it is played out on the faces of those women who watch the film, who incorporate the film into themselves, and who make it part of their lives. And is this not what Kiarostami asks us to do, or what the cinema more generally asks us to do? To make these films parts of our lives, to turn them to our thoughts or into our thoughts, the thoughts that we can live with by virtue of renewing a belief in this world. Right near the end of *Cinema 2* Deleuze evokes such designs:

> There are no longer grounds for talking about a real or possible extension capable of constituting an external world: we have ceased to believe in it, and the image is cut off from the external world. But the internalization or integration of self-awareness in a whole [which is characteristic of the movement-image] has no less disappeared: the relinkage takes place through parcelling [. . .]. This is why thought, as power which has not always existed, is born from an outside more distant than any external world, and, as power which does not yet exist, confronts an inside, an unthinkable or unthought, deeper than any internal world (Deleuze, 1989, pp. 277–8).

With his endings, with his crystalline open images, Kiarostami delivers this 'parcelling' of the external world, the juxtapositions, jumpings and layerings by means of which links can be made precisely as a result of the delinkages between man and the world, between accepted modes of thinking and the external world. The renewed linkages are those between an inside 'deeper than any internal world' – that is, the openness which Kiarostami claims is left to the viewer – but which comes from an outside 'more distant than any external world'; that is, an outside constructed by fabrications, breakages, ellipses and blockages that, in thought beyond accepted thought can come to us. To think in such a way is, for Deleuze, the boldest challenge the cinema can offer.

Notes

Chapter 4

1 Hitchcock's comments are in *Hitchcock/Truffaut*, (Truffaut, 1968, p. 243); cf Modleski, 1988, p. 100, and Pisters, 2003, p. 35.

Chapter 6

1 The quotation from Bergson is from Bergson, 2002, p. 147, p. 149. Ellipses are in Deleuze's original.
2 Fellini's words are from Fellini, 1965, pp. 64–5.

Chapter 7

1 Alain Robbe-Grillet wrote the film's script.

Chapter 8

1 Such links might be made, for example, by a hand, as they are in Bresson (Deleuze, 2006, pp. 315–6).

Chapter 10

1 Italian film actor and director Nanni Moretti asks such questions in his short *The Opening Night of Close-Up* (1996).

Works Cited

Abbas, A. (1997), *Hong Kong: Culture and the Politics of Disappearance*, Minneapolis, MN: University of Minnesota Press.

Aumont, J. (1989), *L'Oeil interminable: Cinéma et pienture*, Paris: Libraire Séguier.

Bassan, R. (2007), 'Three French Neo-Baroque Directors: Beiniex, Besson, Carax from *Diva* to *Le Grand Bleu*', in S. Hayward and P. Powrie (eds), *The Films of Luc Besson: Master of Spectacle*, Manchester: Manchester University Press, pp. 11–22.

Bazin, A. (1971a), 'An Aesthetic of Reality: Cinematic Realism and the Italian School of the Liberation', in *What is Cinema? Volume II*, trans. H. Gray, Berkeley, Los Angeles and London: University of California Press, pp. 16–40.

—. (1971b), '*Umberto D*: A Great Work', in *What is Cinema? Volume II*, trans. H. Gray, Berkeley, Los Angeles and London: University of California Press, pp. 79–82.

Bergala, A. (1999) *Nul mieux que Godard*, Paris: Cahiers du cinema.

Bergson, H. (1988), *Matter and Memory*, trans. N. M. Paul and W. S. Palmer, New York: Zone Books.

Bogue, R. (2003), *Deleuze on Cinema*, New York and London: Routledge.

Bondanella, P. (1992), *The Cinema of Federico Fellini*, Princeton: Princeton University Press.

Bonitzer, P. (1982), *Le champ aveugle: Essais sur le cinema*. Paris: Gallimard.

Bordwell, D. (1982), 'Textual Analysis, etc.', *Enclitic* 5–6, pp. 125–136.

—. (2002), 'Intensified Continuity: Visual Style in Contemporary American Film', *Film Quarterly* 55(3), pp. 16–28.

Brunette, P. (1998), *The Films of Michelangelo Antonioni*, Cambridge: Cambridge University Press.

Buckland, W. (2006), *Directed by Steven Spielberg: Poetics of the Contemporary Hollywood Blockbuster*, New York: Continuum.

Chaudhuri, S. and Finn, H. (2003), 'The Open Image: Poetic Realism and the New Iranian Cinema', *Screen* 44(1), pp. 38–57.

DeBord, G. (1994), *Society of the Spectacle*, New York: Zone Books.

Deleuze, G. (1984), *Kant's Critical Philosophy: The Doctrine of the Faculties*, trans. H. Tomlinson, B. Habberjam, London: Athlone.

—. (1986), *Cinema 1: The Movement-Image*, trans. H. Tomlinson and B. Habberjam, London: Athlone.

—. (1988), *Spinoza: Practical Philosophy*, trans. R. Hurley, San Francisco: City Lights Books.

—. (1989), *Cinema 2: The Time-Image*, trans. H. Tomlinson and R. Galeta, London: Athlone.

—. (1992), *Expressionism in Philosophy: Spinoza*, trans. M. Joughin, New York: Zone Books.

—. (1995), 'Control and Becoming', in *Negotiations*, trans. M. Joughin, New York: Coumbia University Press, pp. 169–176.

—. (1998a), 'To Have Done with Judgment', in *Essays Critical and Clinical*, trans. D. W. Smith and M. A. Greco, London: Verso.

—. (1998b), 'Bartleby; or, The Formula', in *Essays Critical and Clinical*, trans. D. W. Smith and M. A. Greco, London: Verso, pp. 68–90.

—. (2006), 'What is the Creative Act?', in D. Lapoujade (ed.), *Two Regimes of Madness: Texts and Interviews, 1975–1995*, New York: Semiotext(e).

—. and Guattari, F. (1987), *A Thousand Plateaus: Capitalism and Schizophrenia*, trans. B. Massumi, Minneapolis: University of Minnesota Press.

Editors of *Cahiers du Cinéma* (1976), 'John Ford's *Young Mr. Lincoln*', in B. Nichols (ed.), *Movies and Methods Volume I*, Los Angeles, CA: University of California Press, pp. 493–529.

Eisenstein, S. (1963), 'Film Form: New Problems', in Jay Leyda (ed.), *Film Form: Essays in Film Theory*, London: Dennis Dobson.

—. (1970), 'Organic Unity and Pathos in the Composition of *Potemkin*', in *Notes of a Film Director*, New York: Dover, pp. 53–61.

—. (1988a), 'The Dramaturgy of Film Form (A Dialectical Approach to Film Form)', in R. Taylor (ed.), *Selected Works, Volume 1: Writings, 1922–1934*, London: BFI, pp. 161–180.

—. (1988b), 'The Fourth Dimension in Cinema', in R. Taylor (ed.), *Selected Works, Volume 1: Writings, 1922–1934*, London: BFI, pp. 181–194.

Fellini, F. (1965), 'The Long Interview: Tulio Kezich and Federico Fellini', in T. Kezich (ed.), *Federico Fellini's 'Juliet of the Spirits'*, New York: Orion Press.

Foucault, M. (1977), *Discipline and Punish: The Birth of the Prison*, trans. A. Sheridan, London: Allen Lane.

Friedman, L. D. (2006), *Citizen Spielberg*, Urbana: University of Illinois Press.

Gunning, T. (1991), *D. W. Griffith and the Origins of American Narrative Film: The Early Years at Biograph*, Urbana: University of Illinois Press.

—. (2000), *The Films of Fritz Lang: Allegories of Vision and Modernity*, London: BFI.

Jameson, F. (1991), *Postmodernism, Or the Cultural Logic of Late Capitalism*, Durham: Duke University Press.

—. (1992), 'Reification and Utopia in Mass Culture', in *Signatures of the Visible*, New York: Routledge.

Kant, I. (1987) *Critique of Judgment*, trans. Werner S. Pluhar, Indianpolis, IN: Hackett Publishing.

Klein, Melanie, 'Notes on *Citizen Kane*', in J. Philips and L. Stonebridge, *Reading Melanie Klein,* London: Routledge, 1998, pp. 246–250.

Kracauer, S. (1947), *From Caligari to Hitler: A Psychological History of the German Film*, Princeton: Princeton University Press.

Le Roux, H. (1985), 'Le trou de la vierge, ou Marie telle que Jeannot le peint', *Cahiers di cinema* 367, pp. 11–13.

Maratti, P. (2008), *Gilles Deleuze: Cinema and Philosophy*, trans. A. Hartz, Baltimore: The Johns Hopkins University Press.

Modleski, T. (1988), *The Women Who Knew Too Much: Hitchcock and Feminist Theory*, New York: Methuen.

Morrey, D. (2005), *Jean-Luc Godard*, Manchester: Manchester University Press.

Mullarkey, J. (1999), *Bergson and Philosophy*, Edinburgh: Edinburgh University Press.

Nettlebeck, C. (2001), 'Trans-figurations: Verbal and Visual *frissons* in France's Millennial Change', *Australian Journal of French Studies* 39(1), pp. 86–101.

Olkowski, D. (1999), *Gilles Deleuze and the Ruin of Representation*, Berkeley, Los Angeles, London: University of California Press.

Péguy, C. (1932), *Clio*, Paris: Gallimard.

Pisters, P. (2003), *The Matrix of Visual Culture: Working with Deleuze in Film Theory*, Stanford, CA: Stanford University Press.

—. (1997), '*Subway*: Identity and Inarticulacy', in P. Powrie (ed.), *French Cinema in the 1980s: Nostalgia and the Crisis of Masculinity*, Oxford: Clarendon Press, pp. 121–129.

—. (2007), 'Of Suits and Men in the Films of Luc Besson', in S. Hayward and P. Powrie (eds.), *The Films of Luc Besson: Master of Spectacle*, Manchester: Manchester University Press, pp. 75–90.

Proust, M. (1992), *Swann's Way: In Search of Lost Time Volume 1*, trans. C. K. Scott Moncreiff and T. Kilmartin, New York: Random House.

Rancière, J. (2010a), 'The Last Enemy', *Chronicles of Consensual Times*, trans. S. Corcoran, New York: Continuum, pp. 16–19.

—. (2010b), 'The Ethical Turn of Aesthetics and Politics', in *Aesthetics and its Discontents*, trans. S. Corcoran, Cambridge: Polity.

Rodowick, D. N. (1997), *Gilles Deleuze's Time Machine*, Durham, London: Duke University Press.

Rohdie, S. (1990), *Antonioni*, London: BFI.

Rushton, R. (2011a), *The Reality of Film: Theories of Filmic Reality*, Manchester: Manchester University Press.

—. (2011b), 'A Deleuzian Imaginary: The Films of Jean Renoir', *Deleuze Studies* 5(2), pp. 241–260.

Schefer, J. L. (1980), *L'homme imaginaire du cinema*, Paris: Gallimard.

Smith, M. (2003), 'Lars von Trier; Sentimental Surrealist', in M. Hjort and S. MacKenzie (eds.), *Purity and Provocation: Dogma 95*, London: BFI, pp. 111–121.

—. (2008), 'Funny Games', *Dekalog* 1, pp. 117–140.

Sterritt, D. (1999), *The Films of Jean-Luc Godard*, Cambridge: Cambridge University Press.

Truffaut, F. (1968), *Hitchcock/Truffaut*, London: Secker & Warburg.

von Trier, L. (2003a), *Trier on Von Trier*, S. Björkman (ed.), trans. N. Smith, London: Faber and Faber.

—. (2003b), *Lars von Trier Interviews*, J. Humboldt (ed.), Jackson: University of Mississippi Press.

Wilson, E. (2006), *Alain Resnais*, Manchester: Manchester University Press.

Wood, R. (2009), '*Strangers on a Train*', in M. Deutelbaum and L. Poague (Eds.), *A Hitchcock Reader* (second edition), Oxford: Blackwell, pp. 172–181.

Worringer, W. (1957), *Form in Gothic*, trans. H. Read. London: Tiranti.

Filmography

8½ (1963, dir. Federico Fellini, Italy/France)
10 (2002, dir. Abbas Kiarostami, France/Iran/USA)
39 Steps, The (1935, dir. Alfred Hitchcock, UK)
Alien (1979, dir. Ridley Scott, USA/UK)
Alien 3 (1993, dir. David Fincher, USA)
Alien: Resurrection (1997, dir. Jean-Pierre Jeunet, USA)
Aliens (1986, dir. James Cameron, USA/UK)
All the President's Men (1976, dir. Alan J. Pakula, USA)
America America (1963, dir. Elia Kazan, USA)
Amistad (1997, dir. Steven Spielberg, USA)
Anderson Tapes, The (1971, dir. Sidney Lumet, USA)
As Tears Go By (1988, dir. Wong Kar-wai, Hong Kong)
Ashes of Time (1994, Wong Kar-wai, Hong Kong/Taiwan)
Bande à part (1964, dir. Jean-Luc Godard, France)
Battleship Potemkin, The (1925, dir. Sergei Eisenstein, USSR)
Bête Humaine, La (1938, dir. Jean Renoir, France)
Bicycle Thieves (1948, dir. Vittorio De Sica, Italy)
Big Blue, The (1988, dir. Luc Besson, France/USA/Italy)
Big Sky, The (1952, dir. Howard Hawks, USA)

Birds, The (1963, dir. Alfred Hitchcock, USA)
Birth of a Nation, The (1915, dir. D. W. Griffith, USA)
Blair Witch Project, The (1999, dir. Daniel Myrick and Eduardo Sanchéz, USA)
Blow-Up (1966, dir. Michelangelo Antonioni, UK/Italy/USA)
Book of Mary, The (dir. Anne-Marie Miéville, France/Switzerland, 1985)
Breaking the Waves (1996, dir. Lars von Trier, Spain/Denmark/Sweden/ France/Netherlands/Norway/Iceland)
Breathless (1960, dir. Jean-Luc Godard, France)
Broken Blossoms (1919, dir. D. W. Griffith, USA)
Buffalo Bill and the Indians, or Sitting Bull's History Lesson (1976, dir. Robert Altman, USA)
Cabinet of Dr Caligari, The (1920, dir. Robert Weine, Germany)
Cape Fear (1991, dir. Martin Scorsese, USA)
Casino (1995, dir. Martin Scorsese, USA)
Catch Me If You Can (2002, dir. Steven Spielberg, USA)
Certified Copy (2010, dir. Abbas Kiarostami, France/Italy/ Belgium)
Chinoise, La (1967, dir. Jean-Luc Godard, France)
Chronicle of a Summer (1961, dir. Jean Rouch and Edgar Morin, France)
Chunking Express (1994, dir. Wong Kar-wai, Hong Kong)
Citizen Kane (1941, dir. Orson Welles, USA)
Close Encounters of the Third Kind (1977, dir. Steven Spielberg, USA)
Close-Up (1990, dir. Abbas Kiarostami, Iran)
Color of Money, The (1986, dir. Martin Scorsese, USA)
Color Purple, The (1985, dir. Steven Spielberg, USA)
Conversation, The (1974, dir. Francis Ford Coppola, USA)
Corner in Wheat, A (1909, dir. D. W. Griffith, USA)
Dancer in the Dark (2000, dir. Lars von Trier, Spain/Argentina/Denmark/ Germany/Netherlands/Italy/USA/UK/France/Sweden/Finland/Iceland/ Norway)
Day the Earth Stood Still, The (1951, dir. Robert Wise, USA)
Departed, The (2006, dir. Martin Scorsese, USA)
Discreet Charm of the Bourgeoisie, The (1972, dir. Luis Buñuel, France/ Italy/Spain)
Dog Day Afternoon (1975, dir. Sidney Lumet, USA)
Dogville (2003, dir. Lars von Trier, Denmark/Sweden/UK/France/ Germany/Netherlands/Norway/Finland)
Dr Mabuse: The Gambler (1922, dir. Fritz Lang, Germany)
Duel (1971, dir. Steven Spielberg)
E.T.: The Extra-Terrestrial (1982, dir. Steven Spielberg, USA)
East of Eden (1955, dir. Elia Kazan, USA)
Easy Rider (1969, dir. Dennis Hopper, USA)
Element of Crime, The (1984, dir. Lars von Trier, Denmark)

Europa (1991, dir. Lars von Trier, Spain/Denmark/Sweden/France/ Germany/ Switzerland)
Europa '51 (1952, dir. Roberto Rossellini, Italy)
F for Fake (1973, dir. Orson Welles, France/Iran/West Germany)
Fifth Element, The (1997, dir. Luc Besson, France)
Five Obstructions, The (2003, dir. Lars von Trier, Denmark/Switzerland/ Belgium/France)
For Ever Mozart (1996, dir. Jean-Luc Godard, France/Switzerland)
Foreign Correspondent (1940, dir. Alfred Hitchcock, USA)
Fort Apache (1948, dir. John Ford, USA)
Francesco, giullare di Dio (1950, dir. Roberto Rossellini, Italy)
Gangs of New York (2002, dir. Martin Scorsese, USA)
General Line, The (AKA Old and New) (1929, dir. Sergei Eisenstein, USSR)
Gentleman's Agreement (1947, dir. Elia Kazan, USA)
Gentlemen Prefer Blondes (1953, dir. Howard Hawks, USA)
Germany, Year Zero (1948, dir. Roberto Rossellini, Italy)
Giulietta degli spiriti (1965, dir. Federico Fellini, Italy/France)
Godfather, The (1972, dir. Francis Ford Coppola, USA)
Goodfellas (1990, dir. Martin Scorsese, USA)
Happy Together (1997, dir. Wong Kar-wai, Hong Kong)
Helas pour moi (1993, dir. Jean-Luc Godard, France/Switzerland)
Hiroshima, mon amour (1959, dir. Alain Resnais, France/Japan)
Idiots, The (1998, dir. Lars von Trier, Spain/Denmark/Sweden/France/ Netherlands/Italy)
In Praise of Love (2001, dir. Jean-Luc Godard, France/Switzerland)
In the Mood for Love (2000, Wong Kar-wai, Hong Kong/France)
Inception (2010, dir. Christopher Nolan, USA/UK)
Independence Day (1996, dir. Roland Emmerich, USA)
Indiana Jones and the Kingdom of the Crystal Skull (2008, dir. Steven Spielberg, USA)
Indiana Jones and the Last Crusade (1989, dir. Steven Spielberg, USA)
Indiana Jones and the Temple of Doom (1984, dir. Steven Spielberg, USA)
Intolerance (1916, dir. D. W. Griffith, USA)
Invasion of the Body Snatchers (1956, dir. Don Siegal, USA)
Jaws (1975, dir. Steven Spielberg, USA)
Je vous salue, Marie (1985, dir. Jean-Luc Godard, France/Switzerland/UK)
Jurassic Park (1993, dir. Steven Spielberg, USA)
King of Comedy (1982, dir. Martin Scorsese, USA)
Lady from Shanghai, The (1947, dir. Orson Welles, USA)
L'avventura (1960, dir. Michelangelo Antonioni, Italy/France)
L'eclisse (1962, dir. Michelangelo Antonioni, Italy/France)
Last Laugh, The (1924, dir. F. W. Murnau, Germany)

Last Year in Marienbad (1961, dir. Alain Resnais, France/Italy)
Le Mépris (1963, dir. Jean-Luc Godard, France/Italy)
Leon (1994, dir. Luc Besson, France)
Leopard, The (1963, dir. Luchino Visconti, Italy/France)
Letter from an Unknown Woman (1948, dir. Max Ophüls, USA)
Life and Nothing More … (1992, dir. Abbas Kiarostami, Iran)
Lola Montès (1955, dir. Max Ophüls, France/West Germany/
    Luxembourg)
M (1931, dir. Fritz Lang, Germany)
Made in USA (1966, dir. Jean-Luc Godard, France)
Man Who Knew Too Much, The (1956, dir. Alfred Hitchcock, USA)
Man Who Shot Liberty Valance, The (1962, dir. John Ford, USA)
Manchurian Candidate, The (1962, dir. John Frankenheimer, USA)
Manderlay (2005, dir. Lars von Trier, Denmark/Sweden/Netherlands/
    France/Germany/UK/Italy)
Married Woman, A (1964, dir. Jean-Luc Godard, France)
Marseillaise, La (1938, dir. Jean Renoir, France)
Masculin Féminin (1966, dir. Jean-Luc Godard, France/Sweden)
Matrix, The (1999, dir. Wachowski brothers, USA/Australia)
McCabe and Mrs Miller (1971, dir. Robert Altman, USA)
Mean Streets (1973, dir. Martin Scorsese, USA)
Metropolis (1927, dir. Fritz Lang, Germany)
Minority Report (2002, dir. Steven Spielberg, USA)
Moment of Innocence, A (1996, dir. Mohsen Makhmalbaf, Iran/France)
Mon oncle d'Amérique (1980, dir. Alain Resnias, France)
Mr Arkadin (1955, dir. Orson Welles, France/Spain/Switzerland)
Mr and Mrs Smith (1941, dir. Alfred Hitchcock, USA)
Müde Tod, Der (1921, dir. Fritz Lang, Germany)
Muriel, or the Time of Return (1963, dir. Alain Resnais, France/Italy)
Napoléon (1927, dir. Abel Gance, France)
Nashville (1975, dir. Robert Altman, USA)
Network (1976, dir. Sidney Lumet, USA)
Nibelungen, Die ('Siegfried' and 'Kreimhilde's Revenge') (1924, dir. Fritz
    Lang, Germany)
Nikita (1990, dir. Luc Besson, France/Italy)
North by Northwest (1959, dir. Alfred Hitchcock, USA)
Nosferatu (1922, dir. F.W. Murnau, Germany)
Notorious (1946, dir. Alfred Hitchcock, USA)
Notte, La (1961, dir. Michelangelo Antonioni, Italy/France)
October (1928, dir. Sergei Eisenstein, USSR)
On the Waterfront (1954, dir. Elia Kazan, USA)
Opening Night of Close-Up, The (1996, dir. Nanni Moretti, Italy/France)
Passion (1982, dir. Jean-Luc Godard, France/Switzerland)

Pierrot le fou (1965, dir. Jean-Luc Godard, France/Italy)
Prénom Carmen (1983, dir. Jean-Luc Godard, France)
Psycho (1960, dir. Alfred Hitchcock, USA)
Raging Bull (1980, dir. Martin Scorsese, USA)
Raiders of the Lost Ark (1981, dir. Steven Spielberg, USA)
Rear Window (1954, dir. Alfred Hitchcock, USA)
Rebecca (1940, dir. Alfred Hitchcock, USA)
Règle du jeu, La (1939, dir. Jean Renoir, France)
Roma (1972, dir. Federico Fellini, Italy/France)
Ronde, La (1950, dir. Max Ophüls, France)
Roue, La (1923, dir. Abel Gance, France)
Salaam Cinema (1995, dir. Mohsen Makhmalbaf, Iran)
Sauve qui peut (la vie) (1980, dir. Jean-Luc Godard, France/West
    Germany/Austria/Switzerland)
Saving Private Ryan (1998, dir. Steven Spielberg, USA)
Scarface (1932, dir. Howard Hawks, USA)
Schindler's List (1993, dir. Steven Spielberg, USA)
Searchers, The (1956, dir. John Ford, USA)
Sergeant Rutledge (1960, dir. John Ford, USA)
Serpico (1973, dir. Sidney Lumet, USA)
Shirin (2008, dir. Abbas Kiarostami, Iran)
Shutter Island (2010, dir. Martin Scorsese, USA)
Splendor in the Grass (1961, dir. Elia Kazan, USA)
Stagecoach (1939, dir. John Ford, USA)
Star Wars (1977, dir. George Lucas, USA)
Strangers on a Train (1951, dir. Alfred Hitchcock, USA)
Streetcar Named Desire, A (1951, dir. Elia Kazan, USA)
Strike (1925, dir. Sergei Eisenstein, USSR)
Subway (1985, dir. Luc Besson, France)
Suspicion (1941, dir. Alfred Hitchcock, USA)
Taste of Cherry, The (1997, dir. Abbas Kiarostami, France/Iran)
Taxi Driver (1976, dir. Martin Scorsese, USA)
Terminal, The (2004, dir. Steven Spielberg, USA)
Terminator, The (1984, dir. James Cameron, UK/USA)
Terminator 2: Judgment Day (1991, dir. James Cameron, USA/France)
Terminator 3: Rise of the Machines (2003, dir. Jonathan Mostow, USA/
    Germany/UK)
Terminator Salvation (2009, dir. McG, USA/Germany/UK/Italy)
Testament of Dr Mabuse, The (1933, dir. Fritz Lang, Germany)
Thing From Another World, The (1951, dir. Christian Nyby, USA)
Through the Olive Trees (1994, dir. Abbas Kiarostami, France/Iran)
Touch of Evil (1958, dir. Orson Welles, USA)
Triumph of the Will (1935, dir. Leni Riefenstahl, Germany)
Trouble with Harry, The (1955, dir. Alfred Hitchcock, USA)

Two or Three Things I Know About Her (1967, dir. Jean-Luc Godard, France)
Verdict, The (1982, dir. Sidney Lumet, USA)
Vertigo (1958, dir. Alfred Hitchcock, USA)
Viva Zapata! (1952, dir. Elia Kazan, USA)
Vivre sa vie (1962, dir. Jean-Luc Godard, France)
War of the Worlds (2005, dir. Steven Spielberg, USA)
Way Down East (1920, dir. D. W. Griffith, USA)
Weekend (1967, dir. Jean-Luc Godard, France/Italy)
Where is the Friend's House? (1987, dir. Abbas Kiarostami, Iran)
Wild River (1960, dir. Elia Kazan, USA)
Wind Will Carry Us, The (1999, dir. Abbas Kiarostami, Iran/France)
Woman is a Woman, A (1961, dir. Jean-Luc Godard, France/Italy)
Wrong Man, The (1956, dir. Alfred Hitchcock, USA)
Young and Innocent (1937, dir. Alfred Hitchcock, UK)
Young Mr Lincoln (1939, dir. John Ford, USA)

Index